History of Hawaii

A Captivating Guide to Hawaiian History

© Copyright 2022

All Rights Reserved. No part of this book may be reproduced in any form without permission in writing from the author. Reviewers may quote brief passages in reviews.

Disclaimer: No part of this publication may be reproduced or transmitted in any form or by any means, mechanical or electronic, including photocopying or recording, or by any information storage and retrieval system, or transmitted by email without permission in writing from the publisher.

While all attempts have been made to verify the information provided in this publication, neither the author nor the publisher assumes any responsibility for errors, omissions or contrary interpretations of the subject matter herein.

This book is for entertainment purposes only. The views expressed are those of the author alone, and should not be taken as expert instruction or commands. The reader is responsible for his or her own actions.

Adherence to all applicable laws and regulations, including international, federal, state and local laws governing professional licensing, business practices, advertising and all other aspects of doing business in the US, Canada, UK or any other jurisdiction is the sole responsibility of the purchaser or reader.

Neither the author nor the publisher assumes any responsibility or liability whatsoever on the behalf of the purchaser or reader of these materials. Any perceived slight of any individual or organization is purely unintentional.

Free Bonus from Captivating History (Available for a Limited time)

Hi History Lovers!

Now you have a chance to join our exclusive history list so you can get your first history ebook for free as well as discounts and a potential to get more history books for free! Simply visit the link below to join.

Captivatinghistory.com/ebook

Also, make sure to follow us on Facebook, Twitter and Youtube by searching for Captivating History.

Contents

INTRODUCTION 1
CHAPTER 1 - INTRODUCTORY OVERVIEW 3
CHAPTER 2 - ANCIENT HAWAIʻI: THE PEOPLE OF HAWAIʻI 10
CHAPTER 3 - ANCIENT HAWAIʻI: THE GODS AND MYTHS OF HAWAIʻI 28
CHAPTER 4 - POINT OF CONTACT 41
CHAPTER 5 - THE KINGDOM OF HAWAIʻI 55
CHAPTER 6 - THE UNITED STATES AND HAWAIʻI 70
CHAPTER 7 - WORLD WAR II AND HAWAIʻI 88
CHAPTER 8 - MODERN HAWAIʻI 101
CHAPTER 9 - NOTABLE PEOPLE OF HAWAIʻI 113
CHAPTER 10 - CULTURE OF HAWAIʻI 126
CONCLUSION 141
HERE'S ANOTHER BOOK BY CAPTIVATING HISTORY THAT YOU MIGHT LIKE 143
FREE BONUS FROM CAPTIVATING HISTORY (AVAILABLE FOR A LIMITED TIME) 144
REFERENCES 145

Introduction

This book contains a curated walkthrough of the history of Hawaiʻi from the very beginnings of its ancient seafaring ways to the modern incarnation of the US state. Much has happened within this timeframe, and the adventures of Hawaiʻi's people, legends, and culture are a sight to behold. Explanations have been included wherever pertinent, and a reader should have no problem using this book as a starting point to dive into the rich history of this region.

This book traces a path through Hawaiʻi's ideology and religious thoughts, which is unique but also severely underrepresented in mainstream media depictions of the region. This book also chronicles the rise of the Hawaiian kings of old, which occurred both as a natural response to maintain order and as part of the evolution to make contact with the outside world. For many reasons, Hawaiʻi had long been isolated from the emerging cultures and superpowers of the world, and now its footsteps through time are being illuminated. Hawaiʻi had a tumultuous role to play during the Second World War, with a pivotal event occurring on its soil. However, as you will learn in this book, this event did not occur out of the blue. Within these chapters lies the story of the slow and inevitable build-up of tensions and competing national interests that ultimately resulted in "a day that will live in infamy."

Even after such an event, Hawai'i managed to move on, heal, and synthesize an identity that literally and figuratively draws from both ends of the Pacific Ocean and from within the islands themselves to forge a modern state that has gifted the world with brilliant people. In fact, some of them are featured in this book. There will be a detailed look into their lives and accomplishments, which are, for the most part, set against the backdrop of Hawai'i. Additionally, this book offers a truer sense of what is behind the things we take as "quintessentially" Hawaiian and also takes a look into some of the challenges of modern Hawai'i.

As you might have already noticed, we have opted to use the traditional spelling of Hawai'i unless it is being used in a proper name, such as the State of Hawaii or the Republic of Hawaii. Hawai'i is spelled with an okina, and it acts as a glottal stop, which is similar to the break in "uh-oh." This means the word should be pronounced as "huh-wah-ee," although the pronunciation "huh-wah-yee" is very common. There is also a great debate over whether the "w" should be pronounced as a "v." Many locals say "ha-vai-ee."

Jump in, and become immersed in a world of lore, tragedy, and, ultimately, triumph. This world of inspiring tales and strange facts has somehow escaped widespread attention and coverage, but that is no longer the case. With this book, readers hold the key to pierce through the mystique and tropical mythos of Hawai'i and unveil the truth.

Chapter 1 – Introductory Overview

No single book can cover the entire breadth and depth of the storied records of Hawaiʻi. The region is so surprisingly rich that in its comparatively short existence of a thousand or so years, multiple shelves full of books would not be enough to describe all that is noteworthy of Hawaiʻi. Thus, this book is meant to serve not just as an overview but also as a selection of events and times in Hawaiʻi's history that are particularly salient, relevant, representative, and well-documented. Great care and attention have been paid to the sources used within this work, along with the portrayal of the region's history. We hope that the book serves as a deeply engaging and refreshing first dive into the history of Hawaiʻi.

To understand the history of Hawaiʻi, one must first be able to picture it geographically. Humanity and the actions of men and women are what usually form the bulk of history, but the location, topography, and climate of Hawaiʻi are not only unique aspects of the state but also critically important factors in its history. Hawaiʻi is located at the eastern end of Oceania, a sub-region that can be divided into Micronesia, a region of islands located north of New Guinea and east of the Philippines; Melanesia, a region including

New Guinea and extending to the east and south of it; and Polynesia, a large, triangular region that is even farther east of Melanesia, with two of its tips extending into the Northern and Southern Hemispheres.

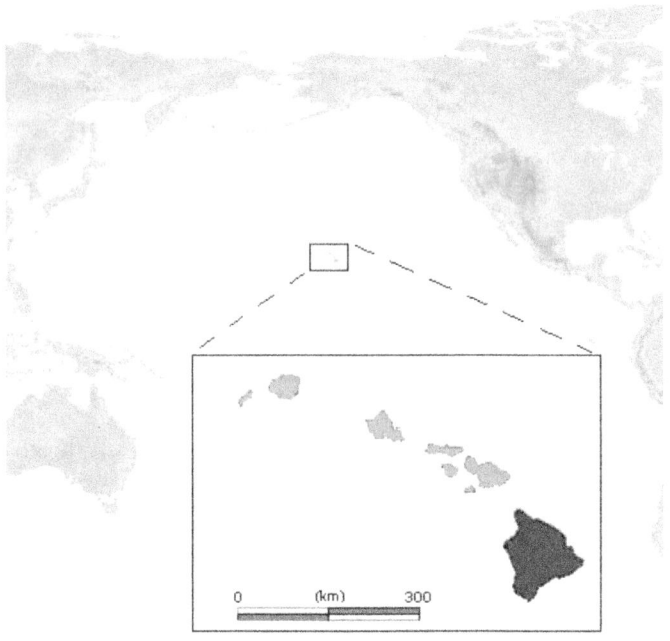

The location of the Hawaiian Islands relative to the Americas on the right and Asia and Australia on the left.
https://commons.wikimedia.org/wiki/File:Hawaii_Islands_-_Hawaii.PNG

At the northern tip of the Polynesian Triangle lies Hawai'i, and even though Hawai'i is nowadays a part of the United States of America, it is the only state that lies outside of North America (although politically it is a part of it). At the other end of the Polynesian Triangle lies New Zealand and Easter Island. Additionally, the State of Hawaii is not a single landmass but rather a group of islands called an archipelago. Hawai'i consists of over one hundred islands, many of which are too small to be properly classified as islands. For most intents and purposes, Hawai'i consists of eight major islands: the island called Hawai'i itself, Maui, O'ahu, Kaua'i, Moloka'i, Lana'i, Ni'ihau, and Kaho'olawe. Together, these eight islands make up more than 90 percent of the emergent land area of the Hawaiian archipelago.

These islands lie about 20 degrees north of the equator in latitude and about 157 degrees west of Greenwich in longitude. This means that Hawai'i experiences a stable and predictable season. Later, we will see how these ideal conditions for agriculture helped steer Hawai'i's history. Their position shows little deviation in seasonal day length as well. This is due to Hawai'i being relatively close to the equator, which means it is not as affected by the sun's yearly north-to-south shift between the tropics of Cancer and Capricorn. The longest summer day in Hawai'i is just over thirteen hours long, and the shortest day is a little under eleven hours long, a minor difference.

Hawai'i, the largest island, bearing the same name as the state itself, has the nickname "the Big Island," and it has a population of around 200,000 people. Maui, the second-largest island, is more than five times smaller than the Big Island, and most of the other islands are comparable in size to Maui. The island of O'ahu, known as "the Gathering Place," actually has the highest population of the eight major islands, with over 900,000 people inhabiting it. Kaua'i is known as "the Garden Isle" due to its extremely fertile lands and history of sugar plantations.

The Hawaiian Islands are home to some of the highest mountains in the world, with Mauna Loa and Mauna Kea rivaling mountains from the Alps. Both are well over four thousand meters (over thirteen thousand feet) high. Although Mauna Kea is now considered a dormant volcano, Mauna Loa is not. In fact, it is still under constant monitoring and surveillance, as it has the potential for hazardous eruptions and is located near populated areas. However, most of Hawai'i's eruptions and volcanic activity aren't overtly dangerous to human or animal life, as its lava flows are usually slow. Due to Hawai'i's isolation from other countries and cities, as well as the sheer height of these two mountains, they are some of the best locations for solar and astronomical observatories.

A panoramic view of the Mauna Kea observatories
Frank Ravizza, CC BY-SA 4.0 <https://creativecommons.org/licenses/by-sa/4.0>, via Wikimedia Commons https://commons.wikimedia.org/wiki/File:Panoroma_of_Mauna_Kea_Observatories.jpg

Hawaiʻi is quite isolated, as it is located near the middle of the Pacific Ocean, far from any major landmasses. This also means that it was far removed from any major centers of civilization, resulting in a culture and people that are truly unique. It has mountainous areas and volcanic activity due to its geological hotspot, which is a unique geological phenomenon due to Hawaiʻi being located far from the edges of its tectonic plate. Most volcanoes occur when tectonic plates diverge away from each other or crush together.

Due to its central location in the Pacific Ocean, Hawaiʻi lies sandwiched between the United States of America and Japan, two powerful nations that have played major roles in charting

Hawaiʻi's course through history. And although this seems like the reason why Captain James Cook, a British explorer and captain in the Royal Navy, eventually named the Hawaiian Islands the "Sandwich Islands," it isn't the real reason. Captain Cook was the first European to document and popularize the trip to the Hawaiian Islands, and he named them in honor of his patron, the Earl of Sandwich, who happened to be the First Lord of the British Admiralty at the time.

The view of Mauna Loa (right) and Mauna Kea (left), as seen and depicted in the 1820s.
https://commons.wikimedia.org/wiki/File:View_of_Hilo,_Mauna_Kea_and_Mauna_Loa_in_the_1820s.jpg

Located north of the equator, Hawai'i is a tropical region, and it maintains a windy and warm climate year-round. Only the tallest mountain areas experience any snowfall, and most of Hawai'i cycles through a wet season and dry season.

Much of Hawai'i's history is influenced by its tropical climate, which allowed for rich agricultural exports and industries. These agricultural revolutions would forever change both the political and ethnic makeup of the islands, attracting global political scrutiny and tens of thousands of migrant labor workers. Later on, these agricultural exports would also go on to shape the world's perception of what "Hawaiian cuisine" was, often erroneously. Interestingly, the surface of the islands of Hawai'i contains an immense range of distinctive features. Hawai'i boasts both windswept, flat beaches and windy, rocky crags. The southern and southeastern slopes of Mauna Loa and Kilauea, two of Hawai'i's active volcanoes, have several long lines of cliffs. These were formed early on when huge portions of the growing mountains slumped into the ocean, either incrementally or suddenly. These ancient, massive landslides sent silt, rock, and volcanic debris tumbling out over the ocean floor for over one hundred miles. These great landslides continue into the present day, with the most recent one occurring in 1975, which triggered an earthquake.

The Hawaiian Islands have both desolate plains of igneous rock and dense, humid rainforests. These mature forests undoubtedly began when algae, lichen, mosses, and ferns began growing on the cooled surface of volcanic basalt and ash. Over time, the weathered rocks and surfaces of the islands would mix with organic material, giving rise to true soil and allowing later stages of floral growth to take root. Hawaiian tarweeds, *Pukiawe*, Hawaiian blueberries, and red tree ferns are just some examples of the many species of vegetation that inhabit the Hawaiian Islands. Hawaiian rainforests also harbor species like *Acacia koa* and *Cheirodendron* (also known as *'olapa*). Hawaiian rainforests are also graded or zoned, mostly according to elevation and other climatic factors. The temperature decreases as the elevation increases, giving rise to floral variation and different kinds of forests. Lowland rainforests are below the mountain rainforests, and both are located below an altitude of 2,000 meters (6,500 feet). This is followed by cool, dry forests and alpine scrub at the higher peaks of Maui and Hawai'i.

These differing climates are due partly to the trade winds that constantly blow against Hawai'i and also partly to the mountainous topography of the islands. These two forces have an interplay between them that allow moisture, rains, storms, and temperatures to fluctuate and stagnate, depending on the location. Notably, the trade winds that come from the east flow over mountains, hills, and valleys to produce drafts and gusts almost all over the islands. A lot of the ocean is cooled by a return current of cold water that runs down from the region of the Bering Straits. Taken together, these mean that the Hawaiian Islands are several degrees cooler than any other island at roughly the same latitude. On the whole, though, Hawai'i's east-facing and west-facing sides are noticeably different. Its eastern sides are windy, rainy, and heavily wooded, with thick forests. The western sides are much sparser in vegetation, being warmer and drier. This difference in plant life is obvious enough to be seen from true color satellite images of Hawai'i.

Hawai'i has a hurricane season that runs from June to November, but the group of islands is buttressed from any real threat by the cooler waters that surround them. Nonetheless, tropical storms are frequent and bring lots of rain, modest winds, and occasionally some property damage.

Significant amounts of metal are rare on the Hawaiian Islands, which meant that Native Hawaiians have had to be very resourceful and creative in finding and utilizing new materials to work with. Most of the major forms of fauna that inhabit the Hawaiian Islands were introduced by the first settlers of the island, who came from New Guinea and parts of Southeast Asia. These animals include dogs, rats, pigs, chickens, and other types of fowl. Notably, of the five species of marine turtles that are found in the central region of the Pacific Ocean, two of them regularly nest on the Hawaiian Islands. One of them is the green sea turtle, or *honu*, and they regularly nest at the smaller, uninhabited northwestern islands of the Hawaiian archipelago. Sometimes, they lay eggs and nest on Moloka'i and even, at least historically, on the island of Lana'i. The other turtle, the hawksbill turtle, or *honu'ea* or simply *ea*, is much less commonly sighted. In the past, its thick shell, which is patterned in an attractive way, was a valuable material to manufacture ornaments from.

For a nation so geographically isolated, Hawai'i is one of the most recognizable and influential island nations in the world, and its deep and diverse history reflects this.

Chapter 2 – Ancient Hawai'i: The People of Hawai'i

Sadly, the earlier histories of Hawai'i are not well documented and have been somewhat eroded due to contact with the outside world. However, lots of evidence, archaeological clues, and connections with the surrounding cultures, peoples, and islands paint a picture that allows us to learn much about the people of ancient Hawai'i.

Origins

Although the exact date of human colonization of the islands of Hawai'i is not accurately known, most scholars and experts on the subject agree that the Polynesian people first set foot on Hawai'i around 900 to 1,100 years ago (around 1100 CE). Prehistoric Polynesians and, by extension, Hawaiians descend from the people of the Lapita culture, named after an archaeological site in New Caledonia (located in the South Pacific). The Lapita people, in turn, seem to have descended from regions of Southeast Asia. Since they are so ancient, one of their more well-known cultural artifacts is a particular type of pottery that has come to be known as Lapita ware, with stamped designs and patterns ringing their bowls and pots. It is very likely that the Lapita people had the hallmarks of many Polynesian peoples. They most likely had adept seafaring skills, utilized various marine resources to the fullest, and had a habit of bringing along animal and plant life, which helped sustain them on new islands.

These ancient Austronesians were skilled sailors, navigators, and explorers, discovering islands to the north, south, and east of modern-day New Guinea and Australia. They progressively moved from one island cluster to another, colonizing inhabitable lands and venturing far out into the Pacific Ocean.

Specifically, the Lapita people spread outward and eastward from the Bismarck Archipelago, located off the northeastern coast of New Guinea, reaching parts of Melanesia around 1250 BCE. Most of their settlements ran along the shores of newly discovered islands, notably not encroaching any great distance farther inland. This prevented them from interacting significantly with any indigenous occupants that might have already populated some of the islands and lands. On the Solomon Islands and some parts of the Bismarck Archipelago, stilt houses were built on the rockier beaches and reef areas.

It is theorized that the Lapita people had an extensive trading network amongst their previous settlements, even though the distance between them would have been quite far. Invariably, the Lapita people would have traded goods and products, which were often sourced from the sea, for other materials and products from people that lived farther upland and inland. This, along with the Lapita people's inhabitance of only coastal areas, would have made them desirable allies and friends. They would have been useful and reliable in providing raw marine resources and other things not available to land-locked communities.

A piece of Lapita pottery found at the Bourewa site in Fiji, approximately three thousand years old.
Patrick Nunn, CC BY-SA 4.0 <https://creativecommons.org/licenses/by-sa/4.0>, via Wikimedia Commons
https://commons.wikimedia.org/wiki/File:Decorated_piece_of_Lapita_pottery_from_the_Bourewa_site_in_Fiji.jpg

Not stopping at Melanesia, the Lapita culture spread out toward the Fiji Islands and even Tonga and Samoa, which lay farther east. This period, approximately around 1000 BCE, marks the oldest estimate of possible incursions into Polynesia. Subtle changes to the shape and designs of the Lapita pottery are able to be progressively tracked and dated, allowing archaeologists to discern their probable movements eastward into Polynesia. Additionally, since these ancient seafarers brought both plants and animals with them to settle onto new islands, modern historians have another angle they can use to track their migration patterns.

The earliest reliable archaeological, linguistic, and animal DNA evidence suggests that Hawaiʻi was discovered and settled from the Marquesas Islands, which lie a little over 3,000 kilometers

(1,860 miles) to the southeast of Hawaiʻi, around 600 CE. Hawaiʻi also had a significant Tahitian influence due to multiple visits to and from the Society Islands, of which Tahiti is a part. These visits and interactions occurred around 1100 CE. In fact, the channel of water that runs from the Hawaiian island of Maui southward that passes between Lanaʻi and Kahoʻolawe is called Kealaikahiki, which literally translates to "the path to Tahiti."

Masters of the Ocean

At some point in time, ancient Austronesian people invented the outrigger canoe, a boat with a single hull that was lashed to smaller wings on either side for added stability, storage, and buoyancy. The exact progression of their inventions and innovations are not known, but there is solid evidence of different forms of these canoes, with some even being fitted with sails for longer journeys. It is also very probable that the peoples of the Lapita culture and the subsequent Polynesians developed the double-hulled canoe and used it for journeys that were hundreds of kilometers long.

Outrigger canoes at Waikiki Beach, circa late 1800s.
https://commons.wikimedia.org/wiki/File:Outrigger_canoes_at_Waikiki_Beach,_late_1800s.jpg

Specifically, ancient Hawaiians used the great endemic Koa trees (*Acacia koa*) to fashion hulls over fifty feet long from a single trunk. They also made other technological advances, such as plating for their wooden hulls, innovations in sail rigging, caulking, and lashing, among other things. These progressive improvements meant that their ships, though wooden, were extremely seaworthy. These large crafts could carry several families, their supplies, domestic animals, and plants to spread on any newly discovered island.

All evidence points to them using celestial navigation and being skilled sailors, repairmen, divers, fishermen, and swimmers. Archaeological and oral traditions tell us that early Hawaiians took their time to perfect and improve their ships and sailing routes. They planned ahead and prepared supplies for long voyages while employing concepts of zenith stars, fixed stars, and seasonal winds for navigation and travel.

The journeys made by ancient Hawaiians and Polynesians were so unbelievably far and dangerous that many anthropologists did not believe the archaeological and linguistic similarities and evidence. In essence, they were convinced that the navigation and technology possessed by the Native Hawaiians were not sufficiently advanced to allow for such journeys. Crossing from the Northern to the Southern Hemisphere also meant that certain celestial navigation tools and techniques would have to be adjusted accordingly and on the fly. This uncertainty stayed ingrained in academic writing and the general consensus for decades.

It was only until Ben Rudolph Finney met Mau Piailug that the debate was truly settled. Ben Finney was an American anthropologist who specialized in surfing, sailing, and navigation. He, along with Herbert Kawainui Kane and Charles Tommy Holmes, founded the Polynesian Voyaging Society, a research and educational society. Mau Piailug was a Micronesian wayfinder who was an expert in non-instrument navigation and open-ocean voyaging, skills that were acquired through rote learning and memorizing the oral traditions of his people. Together with a crew consisting of mostly Native Hawaiians, Finney and Piailug bravely set out on an expedition in 1976, starting from the Hawaiian Islands toward the Society Islands. The ship they used was a double-hulled canoe named *Hokule'a*, which was constructed in a traditional Polynesian design, and they sailed and navigated using only ancient methods. After a month-long voyage, they successfully reached the Society Islands and proved the trip was perfectly possible without the use of modern equipment or navigational methods.

The deck and fabric-sheltered sleeping area of the Hokuleʻa, the double-hulled canoe used to sail from Hawaiʻi to Tahiti.
Tonitt, CC BY-SA 3.0 <https://creativecommons.org/licenses/by-sa/3.0>, via Wikimedia Commons https://commons.wikimedia.org/wiki/File:Hokulea_deck_and_sleeping_area.JPG

Ancient Hawaiians also knew the tides well, correlating them with lunar events and a semidiurnal schedule. Similarly, the occurrence of tsunamis is also posited to be a regular occurrence in prehistoric Hawaiʻi. About every four to five years, a noticeable tsunami would reach the Hawaiian Islands, making a dent in the oral histories and memories of ancient Hawaiians. They would then have stayed away from shores that were prone to tsunami swells, areas like the northeastern coast of Hawaiʻi. Even in recent years, tsunami waves ten meters (thirty-three feet) tall heavily damaged the urban areas of Hawaiʻi. Today, early detection and warning systems are in place to help prevent loss of life and damage.

Food, Flora, and Fauna

The mainstay of ancient Polynesian and Hawaiian diets consisted of starch-rich tubers like the taro plant (*Colocasia esculenta*) and the purple yam or greater yam (*Dioscorea alata*).

Both plants feature prominently in social etiquette, mythology, and rituals. These plants, along with marine animals, formed the main pillars of Native Hawaiian cuisine.

A Hawaiian man transporting harvested taro plants, circa 1898.
https://commons.wikimedia.org/wiki/File:Recueil._%C3%8Eles_Hawa%C3%AF._IV._Culture._Documents_iconographiques_rassembl%C3%A9s_par_Louis_Pierre_Vossion,_Vue_21.jpg

The Kuroshio Current, which runs from the Philippines and the southern Japanese islands, combines with the North Pacific Current to bring most of Hawai'i's marine animals to its archipelago. A similar situation plays out on the southern groups of islands in the Pacific Ocean. Additionally, other marine species would have "island-hopped" their way westward, eventually reaching the Hawaiian archipelago. The coasts of Hawai'i are rich with many different species of seaweeds, corals, mollusks, and bony fish. In all except certain parts of the youngest Hawaiian Islands, living coral reefs surround the coasts of the islands and extend far out into the ocean, becoming more of a "coral-algal" zone farther out. Calling Hawai'i an oasis in the middle of the Pacific Ocean is not an inaccurate statement.

Hawai'i's fish, however, mostly come from the Indo-West Pacific, showing little to no contribution from the eastern side of the Pacific Ocean (the side of the Americas). This is due to much colder currents and an extensive deep-water gap between Hawai'i and the American continents. Some specific examples of Hawai'i's fish are the saddle wrasse or *hinalea lau-wili*, the milletseed butterflyfish or *lau wiliwili*, and the lined coris or *malamalama*. Other nonspecific fish include different types of moray eels, scorpionfishes, groupers, surgeonfishes, jacks, and parrotfishes.

Some of the vitally important plants that were frequently brought over to other islands were the paper mulberry tree, also known as the *tapa* cloth tree (*Broussonetia papyrifera*), the coconut tree, and the palm lily or *ki* tree. The paper mulberry, in particular, was cultivated for its inner bark, which was slowly peeled, soaked, and then beaten to manufacture barkcloth, or *kapa*. Barkcloth was used not only for clothing and decorative purposes but also as tapestries and a form of canvas that was painted on.

An artist's depiction of a Hawaiian woman pounding natural fibers to make the clothes they use to dress themselves, 1819.
Hiart, CC0, via Wikimedia Commons
https://commons.wikimedia.org/wiki/File:%27Woman_of_the_Sandwich_Islands_making_the_Natural_Cloth_with_which_they_are_Dressed%27_by_Jacques_Arago.jpg

Coconut plants would have multiple uses, from building timber to starting fires to creating ropes, which were spun from its fibers. The nutritional content of the coconut also meant that most ancient Polynesians treasured the coconut tree for all its uses, earning it the nickname of "the tree of life." Other plants that ancient Polynesians and Hawaiians would bring along with them included bananas, breadfruit, and Polynesian arrowroot.

Ancient Life

Ancient Hawaiians almost definitely had an agrarian lifestyle and possessed a complex, communal society that included caste systems. The highest rung consisted of chiefs and leaders of villages and regions. Priests, shamans, healers, and professional craftsmen made up the majority of the second rung of the caste system, followed by the common people who made up most of the population. It is also very likely that even in ancient Hawai'i, society was organized around the concept of an extended family unit, the *ohana*. This unit was very important to ancient Hawaiians because it was connected to their caste system, the ruling class, genealogical naming of family gods, and even the ownership of land. Further kinship groups would develop from the *ohana*, and aggregations of these would then form villages or inhabit a region. The overall task of the *ohana* was to cultivate, find, hunt, or harvest food and other raw materials, whether from agricultural or marine sources. These would be used to sustain both the *ohana* and the larger group that it belonged to, along with other requirements of trading, levies, religious offerings, and more.

Although ancient Hawaiian agriculture was not as advanced as other mass-producing agricultural civilizations, it was nonetheless systematic and reliable enough to not only maintain an adequate supply of food but also to grow the population at a steady rate. Such a feat was accomplished not with metal tools or animal-driven implements but rather with a system of work allocation and group effort. There is also evidence of more advanced agricultural constructions and aquaculture practices dating back to the ancient Hawaiians. Freshwater ponds and multilevel terraces were constructed to help crops like taro and sweet potato to grow and flourish.

Meat from swine and fowl would serve only as supplementary food sources and not as the main staples of everyday life. Hunting would very likely be carried out simultaneously alongside gathering, with the activity being one that involved the entire family. Similarly, fishing and marine resource collection was a family affair, especially in the shallower coastal areas. Deepsea fishing would only be done by specialists, as they had to employ large canoes, deep-sea fishing lines, spears, nets, and expert diving and swimming techniques. Old records of oral histories of ancient Hawai'i tell of fleets of canoes going out to sea with many men in a massive effort to catch fish and other marine life. The people would prepare in advance for such expeditions, preparing long braided fishing lines and different types of hooks and spears. Some of the largest nets would hold enough fish that they needed ten to twenty canoes to help bring the catch back to shore.

A manuscript sketch of Hawaiian natives with their animals by Louis Choris, a GermanRussian painter and explorer who was known for his expedition research sketching.
https://commons.wikimedia.org/wiki/File:Hawaiian_natives_wearing_kihei,_with_animals,_sketch_by_Louis_Choris.jpg

Margaret Titcomb, an American librarian who wrote several books on Hawai'i, claims that the dog in the center of the painting is the only depiction of the now-extinct Hawaiian poi dog. (Source: Honolulu Academy of Arts, original work by Louis Choris, 1816) Canoes were critically important in helping secure bountiful harvests of marine protein. These ships would also be used for trading, exploration, settlement of new areas, and religious rituals.

Thus, canoe-making in ancient Hawai'i was a revered and specialized craft. It is known that canoe-making was held in high regard in pre-European Hawai'i, complete with all the attendant concepts and practices of strict apprenticeship and deep mastery, which took years. The work was surrounded by the appropriate ceremonies and rituals that were performed by priests and shamans, from the mere selection of which log was to be felled to the dragging of the finished vessel down to the water.

One of the most alien concepts to Native Hawaiians was that one could possess sources of water like lakes and rivers and the right to their use. Early Hawaiians regarded water as utterly inseparable from the land itself, believing that bodies of water were communally owned. Such an attitude toward the sanctity of water would help explain how large irrigation projects and manmade water streams on the Hawaiian Islands came about, as the amount of labor needed was immense and could only be accomplished through a concerted, collective effort. Writings from old Native Hawaiian farmers state that "Water, then, like sunlight, as a source of life to land and man, was the possession of no man, not even the *ali'i nui* [chiefs] or the *mo'i* [ruler]."

Kings, Rulers, and Commoners

The kinship politics of ancient Hawai'i were headed by high chiefs called *ali'i*. These chiefs would rule over districts of an island along with their families. Leaders that were secondary to the *ali'i* were called *konohiki* and were responsible for overseeing and stewarding the *ahupua'a*. The *ahupua'a* is a section of land on the island that took into consideration access to water, fertile ground, residential areas, high ground, and many other factors in its allotment to a family or group. One way to conceptualize the *ahupua'a* is to visualize a "weirdly-shaped pizza slice" of land from an island that made sure to include all the needs of an *ohana* or village. The *konohiki* were usually distant relatives of the high chiefs and also helped them govern the common people, or *maka'ainana*. Even amongst the *maka'ainana*, there were societal classes and hierarchical divisions.

High chiefs of large districts or even entire islands would be met with respect and prostration; any sign of blatant disrespect was punishable by death. A ruler's clothes could not be worn by common men, and his house was a sacred place where only those who were permitted could enter. A high chief would be attended to and advised by a group of nobles, which traditionally favored the paternal side of the family. Some of the lesser-ranked members of the king's cohort would be responsible for waiting on him, helping him stay cool with fans, bathing and massaging him, and fetching him food and drinks. Other members would be treasurers, heralds, runners, and chief stewards that would report daily activities to the king. Furthermore, the court would consist of storytellers, dancers, musicians, guards, diviners, priests, and wayfinders.

Skilled craftsmen like canoe-makers, healers, and rope and net makers would be ranked the highest amongst the common people, followed by the farmers, workers, and their family members (they made up the largest group of the population). Religious leaders and priests would be individuals held in high esteem regardless of the caste system, as they served the gods and helped bridge the gap between what was man and what was divine. The duties and responsibilities held by the priests were vast. They would hold ceremonies to appease the gods of land and water for agricultural success. They would read signs and advise rulers on auspicious times for harvesting, fishing, sailing, and exploring. They would also help ward off calamitous storms, volcanic activity, disease, and tsunamis. These priests, shamans, and sorcerers were collectively known as *kahuna*. Lastly, as is common with many other civilizations, prisoners of war and criminals were at the bottom of the social ladder, and they were called *kauwa*.

Amongst the commoners, there are two prevailing theories of exactly what the *ohana* included and meant. The first theory speculates that *ohana* referred to all the families that were living in that area. Such a grouping of families would occupy an *ili*, which was a subdivision of the *ahupua'a*. The *ili* would include dry land, wet land, and inhabitable land. The *ohana* living here would pay their taxes to their group's leader, and the amount was calculated in proportion to the land allotted.

Such taxes would invariably contribute to the royal tax, which proceeded in a pyramidal manner upward. The royal tax was mostly made up of articles of food, so there would be bundles of fruit, taro, and sweet potato along with portions of meat from dogs, hogs, fowl, and fish. Other gifts could be precious stones, beautiful shells, rare bird feathers, and polished rock decorations and jewelry. Still, a separate labor tax would also be enacted upon the *maka'ainana*. Some of them would be tasked to tend to the gardens that belonged to the royal family, and others would be sent out for public work like repairing and building temples, advancing irrigation projects, and constructing new houses. Justice would have probably taken the form of a complaint system to family heads, then to the *konohiki*, and perhaps even to the king himself. Legal proceedings wouldn't be much more than sentencing, and petty crimes would see private revenge. More serious crimes were punished by execution, which was carried out by the chiefs' *ila'muku*, or executioner. This ensured a decent level of serious crime deterrence.

The second theory of what *ohana* meant in ancient Hawai'i is that it was not a genealogically driven concept but merely a kindred network. This relaxed definition of a family meant that a group system of cooperation was prioritized and also allowed for shifting access to the land as needs arose. This theory is further supported by the fact that maintaining genealogical lines among the commoners was forbidden by the *ali'i*. Allowing inheritances and rigid notions of the family to take root would have led, and indeed did lead to, conflict and wars.

TATTOOED HAWAIIAN CHIEF, DRAWN BY JACQUES ARAGO, ARTIST WITH FREYCINET.

A depiction of a chief or officer of **King Kamehameha II** in full traditional dress, circa 1819.
https://commons.wikimedia.org/wiki/File:Tattooed_Hawaiian_Chief,_Drawn_by_Jacques_Arago,_Artist_with_Freycinet.jpg

Early on in Hawai'i's development, blood ties would have been the main factor in determining *ohana*. In time, however, only high chiefs and rulers would be allowed genealogical titles of great importance, making marriage within their own families a frequent practice. As time went on, power would be determined by marriages and warfare. Commoners would have little to no property rights that were linked to bloodlines and family possession. The *maka'ainana* would be moved about by war and conquest, maintaining loose ties to extended families. The redistribution of land and reallocation of land stewardship, which would happen after new bouts of conquest, unavoidably shifted these groups around. Defeated rulers would sometimes lose their societal standing and become commoners themselves, but being offered as a sacrifice to the gods was also common for conquered rulers. Sometimes they would even become or choose to become social outcasts or untouchables (*kauwa*).

Although there seems to be little evidence of a distinct warrior class, specially trained military guards were dispatched to guard royalty and lead invasions or defenses against intruders. Most of the people of ancient Hawai'i were trained in the use of weapons and occasionally drilled in groups, where they engaged in mock fights and learned battle techniques. Ancient Hawaiian weapons were similar to the rest of the world, as they used spears, daggers, clubs, slings, and javelins. Notably, Hawaiians did not employ shields of any sort; instead, they resorted to becoming experts in avoiding, catching, and parrying thrown weapons coming at them. Bows and arrows were not widely used in warfare, as they were mostly only utilized in hunting and vermin extermination. Ambush tactics and fights on open fields were the prevailing strategies, but sea battles would sometimes see upward of a hundred canoes on each side clashing. Largescale sea fights were rare, though, due to the amount of preparation, manpower, and materials that were required.

Interestingly, Hawaiian mythology tells of different races of dwarf people, wild hunters, and forest dwellers who lived on the islands before the first people of Hawai'i ever reached land. These people are collectively called Menehune, but no concrete historical evidence of such people has been discovered. In other Central Polynesian islands, the older term *manahune* referred to slaves or workers of a lower social rank and status. It is quite likely that these practices were mostly abandoned in ancient Hawai'i but that the term stuck around. As the tales slowly morphed into legends, the aspect of low social status might have slowly changed over time to refer to the diminutive physical size of the Menehune.

Temples

The ancient people of Hawai'i built elaborate and large temples called *heiau*, many of which were unfortunately destroyed due to pressure from Christian missionaries and Western contact.

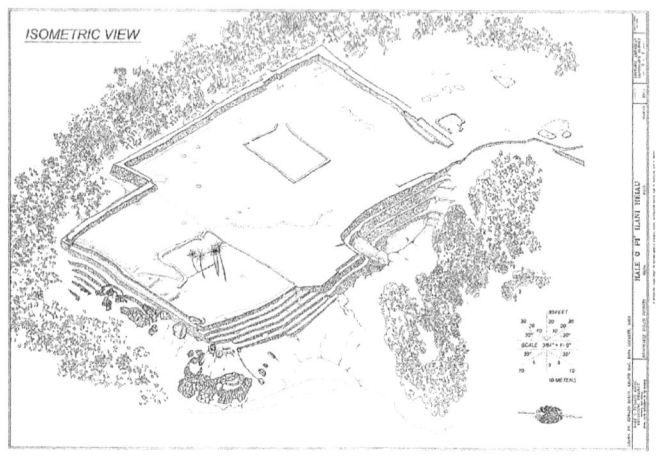

An overhead isometric view of the Hale O Pi'ilani Heiau, Maui. The image shows terraced borders and sectioned parts for different purposes and crowds.
https://commons.wikimedia.org/wiki/File:Hale-o-pi-ilani-heiau.jpg

Most *heiaus* were simple structures, but they were not meant to be works of art. Broken pieces of cooled lava were often found around the sites of older *heiaus*, and water-smoothened pebbles were worked into the mud and onto the floors to ensure a relatively smooth surface upon which to walk and kneel. Grass-thatched huts with massive stone and rock walls would be built on elevated parts of the ground or on terraced ground. Simplicity permeated the images of the gods, sometimes even bordering on the crude. *Heiau* sites were almost invariably walled around, whether in a rectangular layout or a circular one.

Still, some *heiaus* were deliberately elaborate, with the largest ones being many stories tall. They were built primarily with religious purposes in mind. *Heiaus* would be built to venerate the gods, influence the weather, and pray for success in agriculture and war. These structures were made from many different types of materials, including sand, lava rock, sandstone, and coral. In the course of worshiping their many gods, Hawaiians would serve up offerings of incense, fish, meats, sacred barkcloth, fruits, bounties of agricultural harvest, and, during certain times of war, human sacrifices. However, perhaps the most important part of worship was chanting prayers, with the most sacred of these rituals being chanted by a high priest. Scaffolding would be erected within the *heiau*. This structure was called *Lananuʻumamao*, so named because the scaffolding was constructed in three stages: the *nuʻu* (earth), *lani* (heavens), and *mamao* (a faraway place that was within hearing distance). The entire structure would be covered in white barkcloth, and only the more distinguished members of society could "ascend" into the inner parts of the *Lananuʻumamao*. The last and most sacred stage could only be entered by the high priest and the ruling chief. Each step of this scaffolding would have prayers and offerings; it was, in essence, a stage-by-stage ritual that incorporated a series of prayers, images, and other objects, like bent saplings, cords, and drums.

Chapter 3 – Ancient Hawai'i: The Gods and Myths of Hawai'i

Ancient Hawaiians were polytheistic and animistic, with many of their mythological and theological beliefs bleeding into their approaches and ideology toward land ownership, societal norms, sailing practices, farming practices, and warfare. This divine nature was also intensely expressed in their notion of sovereignty, as kings and rulers were believed to be descended from the gods. It was thought they possessed a sacred and religious character. Superstitious awe and ritualistic proceedings would follow new royal births, as well as visits to holy sites, *heiaus*, and volcanic mountains. Legends and myths regularly reference and use lightning and thunder as heralds of an important event. This divine nature would be reflected in their red feather cloaks, helmets, and capes, and only those of royal blood would be permitted to don such clothing.

Firstly, it is important to understand that to capture Hawaiian mythology is to capture the entire range of storytelling that encapsulates folklore, oral traditions, superstitions, prayers, chants, and many other such things. Moreover, such a deep mythology, one that was spread over hundreds of years and over vast distances and different islands, needed to incorporate the culture, economy, and ideology of the ancient Hawaiian people.

Among Hawaiians and even more so for ancient Hawaiians, the usage of the word for god, *akua*, is not fixed and determinate. The word may refer to almost any object of nature, manmade image, or even phenomena of nature. In other words, the gods and mythology of ancient Hawai'i are intrinsically naturalistic and, to some extent, animistic. Another important philosophical concept among ancient Hawaiians is the relation of the individual to the physical universe around them through the use of pairing opposites. The ideas of night and day, light and darkness, male and female, or land and water permeate Hawaiian mythology and the composition of chants.

Gods are often represented in Hawaiian stories as chiefs and lords, and they sometimes dwelled in fantastical lands and abodes in the heavens. Of the great gods that are worshiped, none are mentioned more often than the gods Ku, Kane, Lono, and Kanaloa, as evidenced by multiple early missionary writings and letters. These gods are often invoked together in chants and songs. In fact, the first prayer of some ceremonies is often nothing more than an enumeration and invocation of the numerous names of the god or gods that are being worshiped through that ceremony.

Gods would also have families, so there would be subordinate gods within those families. These "lesser gods" would be invoked by those who hoped to gain something that was specifically associated with the lesser gods, such as certain skills or success in a particular activity. Even thieves had a patron god in Hawaiian mythology. It is probable that the four

"Great Gods" were first conceived of as nature deities with universal significance and powers, only to be associated with particular human beings and human traits later on. This would explain why some Native Hawaiians looked upon Captain James Cook as Lono because they thought the god had returned to them in the form of this impressive, albeit alien, man. In other words, divinity is thought of as lying dormant and being infused with normal, everyday things, such as water. It manifests itself in an obvious physical form only when active. This placed further importance on genealogical descent for ancient Hawaiians.

As is the case with many other cultures, Hawaiian mythology recognizes a period of history before humans when spirits and gods alone populated the seas and the lands. There is a noted absence of detailed primeval or cosmic mythology. Later migrations from Tahiti, which was once called "Kahiki," have also left their mark on chants and legends, which is evidenced by linguistic identities and corresponding forms, such as morphemes, phonologically similar names, etc. The Hawaiians kept their ancestral bonds with Kahiki alive, as they honored them as the progenitor of the family line. Plots of heroic tales and romances trace back to the chiefs in Tahiti.

Kahuna

Even the priests of ancient Hawai'i were divided into several orders, some of which were hereditary in nature. Rote memorization was highly emphasized as the method of teaching and communication, resulting in a special duty for priests. They had to commit to memory the long prayers and naming systems of gods and family gods. Hence, the *kahuna*, besides being the priests and shamans of the islands, were also the learned class of ancient Hawai'i, passing on the accumulated knowledge of astronomy, history, medicine, philosophy, and theology. Later on, the term would change to also encapsulate the meaning of "expert" or refer to someone who is an authority on a subject.

A Hawaiian kahuna, circa 1890.
https://commons.wikimedia.org/wiki/File:Hawaiian_Kahuna_Kahiko_(PP-33-11-023).jpg

Kane

According to the accounts of missionaries and Europeans who first made documented contact with ancient Native Hawaiians, the god Kane was chief amongst their pantheon of gods. Kane was the great god of procreation and was also worshiped as the ancestor of both royalty (chiefs of different levels) and commoners. Kane plays a central figure in both the creation account of the world and in many versions of the Kumu-Honua, the legend of the first man on Earth.

Kane is said to have made three worlds, with the first being the upper heaven, a realm where gods dwell high above the earth. The second world would be the lower heaven, resting just above the earth, a place of the sky, stars, clouds, and rain. The third world would then be the garden of Earth, with mankind and all the animals and plants that were in it. After that, Kane is said to have made man out of a combination of clays. The right side of the man's head was made from clays of the north and east, while the left side of the head was made from clays of the south and west.

Then, working together with the gods Ku and Lono, Kane and Ku breathed into the nostrils of the fashioned man, while Lono breathed into its mouth, thus giving man life. Many accounts of ancient Hawaiian myths and legends have too many similarities with biblical stories to be a coincidence. Indeed, many scholars see these accounts as having been painted with coloring and emphasis that is decidedly Christian, especially since some of the first Europeans who wrote about Native Hawaiian mythology were missionaries. However, after removing elements of Christianity that were probably inadvertently included, these accounts are not too far removed from the truth, as evidenced by their similarities to Tahitian creation myths.

Kane would be worshipped at *heiaus* without images for a long time. Some of the *heiaus* would have stones fashioned into a conical shape representing Kane, possibly with some paintings or carvings to further give the stone character. People would come and offer food and pray for forgiveness for any trespasses they might have made against the laws of the land. The Kane stone is also somewhat related to the shape of the male sexual organ, which is in line with Kane's generative powers over life and humanity. When worshiping Kane, families would have their own *'aumakua* (family god), and it would be reflected in the names of their own Kane god. The variety of these family god names would be extensive, numbering up to the thousands, but they all referred to the one god. Accordingly, in *heiaus*, there was one central altar at which to offer food and prayers.

One example of the myriad forms of Kane worship is the worship of Kane-hekili, meaning "Kane in the thunder." Native Hawaiians would worship Kane-hekili as an *'aumakua* on the island of Maui, along with other gods of thunder and lightning. When a heavy, loud storm would happen, legends say that it was customary to flip all containers upside down and to lie facedown, not making any sound. Silence during such heavy storms was considered the *tapu* (law) of Kane-hekili. Yet another legend tells of Oʻahu's Kaneana Cave, which has two stones resembling humanoid shapes. They are said to be the petrified forms of two boys that disobeyed their mother's instructions of keeping still and silent during the thunderstorm. Such customs would be observed by any family who claimed a thunder *ʻaumakua*, thereby worshiping Kanehekili.

Many chiefs of early Hawaiʻi believe they were descended directly from Kane himself and are of the Ulu or Nanaulu line. These chiefs ranked higher than other chiefs, who had a less distinguished family genealogy. Such prestige came with the power to dictate *tapus* and judge offenses. Sometimes their authority would even approach divine status, and they would hold sway over matters of life and death. They would otherwise be known as *na liʻi kapu akua*, or "chiefs with the tapus of gods."

Ku

Ku and Hina are the male and female forms, respectively, of the great ancestral gods of heaven and Earth. Linguistically, *Ku* means erect and to stand upright, whereas *Hina* means to lean and lay downward. Solar movements can also be labeled with these terms, with the rising sun being referred to as Ku and the setting sun being referred to as Hina.

Therefore, Ku is the expression of male generative power and virility. Hina is seen as the expression of female fertility and the power of growth and production. Together, they make up one inclusive whole, with Ku presiding over all the male spirits and gods and Hina over the female ones. Much like other phallic symbolism, Ku is represented as a pointed and upright stone, a *pohaku*, which has come to mean "stone or rock" in the Hawaiian language today. Hina's primordial female energy is symbolized with a flat, rounded stone that is lying down, which is called *papa*.

Carving of the god Ku in his form of the war-god Ku-kaʻili-moku, meaning "Ku, the Snatcher of Land."
jmcd303, CC BY-SA 2.0 <https://creativecommons.org/licenses/by-sa/2.0>, via Wikimedia Commons https://commons.wikimedia.org/wiki/File:Ku_woodcarving_in_heiau.jpg

The family of gods that are given Ku names are many and cover things like forests, rain, fishing, and war, to name a few. Some examples of these are the god of war, Ku-nui-akea (Ku the supreme one); the god of fishing, Kuʻula (Ku of the bounties of the sea); and the god of the green land, Ku-olono-wao (Ku of the deep forest). The Ku gods of the forest would be worshiped by hunters and gatherers who ventured deep inland to gather wild food in times of scarcity and need. Canoe builders would pray to their canoe-building gods to help them with specific activities or hardships, like hollowing out a canoe with a bevel adze, a carpentry tool.

Kanaloa

While Kanaloa is often mentioned amongst the foremost of the gods of ancient Hawai'i, not much is known about him. Kanaloa is the god of the squid and might be connected to the god that breaks the evil influence of sorcery and black magic. However, Kanaloa is treated with a level of distrust that is uncommon for the chief gods of the Hawaiian pantheon. He is not invoked with the same level of trust and devotion as other 'aumakua, and he is associated with certain qualities of deep and dark water. These qualities smack of uncertainty, danger, dark spirits, death, and other themes of the underworld. Various legends of strife and conflict with the god Kane are told in which Kanaloa and his subordinate spirits rebel against the gods of the sky, Kane in particular.

Although legend places Kane and Kanaloa in opposition as the good and evil gods of mankind, some legends show them as complementary halves of a whole. This is also evidenced by wider genealogies of similar gods across Polynesia, where they also hold dominion over the afterlife. These connections of death and creation show that Kane and Kanaloa were two necessary halves of the world, a philosophy that is not overly concerned with the dichotomy of good versus evil. In cultural activities and old chants, there exists a vast amount of mythical and religious lore that invokes Kane and Kanaloa together. Both gods were invoked by those involved with canoes, whether they were builders, explorers, or sailors, with Kane being for the consecration of newly built canoes and Kanaloa for sailing.

The island of Kaho'olawe is also said to belong to Kanaloa. Some chants and oral histories see the Tahitian god Ta'aroa, the contemporary or origin god of Kanaloa, as landing on the shores of Kaho'olawe and naming the island after himself. Additionally, Kane and Kanaloa are described as avid awa (kava) drinkers and water-finders, explorers, and cultivators of new islands. Mythologically, both Kane and Kanaloa are described as gods who lived in the bodies of men.

Lono

Some scholars believe that Lono was a later fusion of the Tahitian gods Roʻo and Tane, with Roʻo being the messenger of Tane. They were the gods of the sky, clouds, rain, and storms. In Hawaiʻi, Lono is the influencer and master of clouds, thunder, lightning, and whirlwinds. Since the ancient Hawaiians were exposed to many interactions between winds, water, rain, and waves, they drew mythical and meteorological connections between phenomena like waterspouts, mountain springs, and cloud formations. These things were considered to be under the purview of the god Lono. As such, the order of priests worshiping Lono would set up *heiaus* to pray for rain and favorable weather conditions for sailing and fishing. The Lono priests existed well into the days of King Kamehameha, and they built *heiaus* and shrines to pray for deliverance from sicknesses and for abundant rain and crop growth.

A figure depicting the Hawaiian god Lono, circa 1790.
*Sailko, CC BY 3.0 <https://creativecommons.org/licenses/by/3.0>, via Wikimedia Commons
https://commons.wikimedia.org/wiki/File:Hawaii,_figura_del_dio_lono,_1790_ca._01.JPG*

Pele

In 1840, the renowned American geologist James Dana correctly deduced that the islands of Hawai'i were formed from volcanic hotspot activity, with the youngest island being the "Big Island," the island of Hawai'i itself, and the oldest island being the island of

Kauaʻi. He deduced this from observations of the degrees of erosion of volcanic peaks on the islands.

This pattern of decreasing age going from northwest to the southeast of the Hawaiian island chain had already been recognized by ancient Hawaiians and is represented as such in the telling of the Pele legend.

It is said that the volcano goddess Pele and her family came from the land of Kahiki (Tahiti), which was regarded as a faraway mythical land to ancient Hawaiians. In the vein of Hawaiian mythology being centered around families and gods having a certain element that they are intimately connected with, Pele and her family looked to build a home of lava and fire in a volcanic hollow. She began digging on the island her family first landed on, the island of Niʻihau. But for every deep and large hole she dug, groundwater would rush in and flood the pit, rendering it unsuitable for her and her family.

Pele continued with her efforts on all of the islands, making her way southward, only to have her efforts fail again and again. When she reached the island of Hawaiʻi, she was able to find a home for her family in the water-free pits of Mokuʻaweoweo and Halemaʻumaʻu. Pele and her family made their abodes there in fiery homes of lava and magma. Today, those two pits lie in the calderas of Mauna Loa and Kilauea, respectively, with Mauna Loa being the largest active volcano on Earth and Kilauea being Hawaiʻi's most active volcano.

Halemaʻumaʻu crater, Kilauea volcano.
Ivan Vtorov, CC BY-SA 3.0 <https://creativecommons.org/licenses/by-sa/3.0>, via Wikimedia Commons
https://commons.wikimedia.org/wiki/File:Halema%27uma%27u_Crater_in_Kilauea_volcano,_Hawaii..jpg

The volcanic origins of Hawaiʻi have largely been a boon for both ancient and Native Hawaiians. The rich mineral content makes for extremely fertile soil, and volcanic glass was an invaluable resource for ancient Hawaiians, who used the razor-sharp flakes for drills, cutting tools, and various other implements. Archaeological investigations also show that ancient Hawaiians had an extensive mining and quarry site near the southern summit of Mauna Kea, an area rich in fine-grained basalt. These were used to manufacture adze and other similar tools, even though the site was located in a dangerous and inhospitable environment.

Antennae covered with strands that seem like hair at Puʻu Oʻo, near Kilauea, Hawaiʻi. These hairs are thin, hardened strands of volcanic glass. In Hawaiʻi, they are called "lauoho o Pele" or "Pele's hair," and they are named after the goddess.
https://commons.wikimedia.org/wiki/File:Peleshair_on_antenna.jpg

Stones and boulders that resembled male and female genitalia often held special significance for ancient Hawaiians, and a few groupings of large boulders would be recognized as special "birthing stones." They would be visited by pregnant wives of chiefs and other pregnant female royalty. Oral traditions tell of how they would lay on top of these stones or touch and worship them to bring good fortune and health to both themselves and their babies. Such associations of formations of rocks and stones with deities and lesser gods were common in early Hawaiʻi. Some even formed the site of religious shrines, and other large stones were known as "bell stones," which would ring out sonorous tones when struck.

Chapter 4 – Point of Contact

Hawai'i's historical trajectory changed dramatically upon its contact with European explorers, which began with the arrival of British explorer Captain James Cook in 1778. Despite this being the most well-known and well-documented instance of Hawaiian contact with European travelers, Spanish archives have documentation of a fleet of conquistador ships sailing from the southern end of Mexico toward the Philippines that arrived at islands that resemble Hawai'i. Nonetheless, these findings and discoveries were not publicized or made widely known by Spain. In all likelihood, Spain kept the discovery of the Hawaiian Islands a secret to maintain supremacy over trading lines and to retain a naval advantage.

James Cook Arrives

Contested claims aside, James Cook is generally credited as being the first European to "discover" Hawai'i, and he made two trips to the island. He had already made two voyages around the globe, and on December 8th, 1777, he captained two armed ships, the *Discovery* and *Resolution*, to set out for the northwest coast of North America from the Society Islands, where Tahiti is. A month later, in January of 1778, James Cook landed on O'ahu and spotted the island of Kaua'i just ahead. The following days saw him sail toward Ni'ihau, and he eventually came into contact with local

Hawaiians on the southeastern side of Kauaʻi. The locals and James Cook bartered and exchanged vegetables and fish for nails and metal. Captain Cook was surprised by their friendliness and ability to speak a language not so different from the one spoken on the Society Islands.

Slowly, as the ships proceeded toward more agreeable coasts, the news spread amongst the natives, and excitement grew. James Cook made a note of large crowds of people gathering to see the novel sight of his ships, himself, and the other strange visitors. Upon trying to go ashore with three armed boats, some locals pressed onto James Cook's group too thickly and tried to take away their oars, muskets, and anything else that seemed interesting and modern. Cook's entourage was forced to fire a warning shot, killing one man but restoring a boundary of personal space between them and the natives in the process.

Eventually, the natives came to revere and even worshiped Captain Cook and his men, as they were seen as kings or beings with divine authority. When Captain Cook and his boats anchored at Waimea Bay, the natives brought forth offerings of captured pigs and plantain trees, and prayers were performed by priests and shamans. In return, Captain Cook gave them nails, knives, pieces of iron, and cloth, which pleased the natives greatly, as iron was a scarce resource and was seen as a precious metal. In fact, even sacred red feathers and cloaks that were reserved for royalty were offered to Captain Cook.

Eventually, he ventured inland with a few men, including his surgeon and the expedition's artist. He was followed by a train of natives, and he eventually walked up a valley to visit a *heiau*, of which he wrote descriptions and asked for a drawing to be made. Over the following days, Cook would visit the islands of Niʻihau and Kauaʻi. As he was leaving Kauaʻi, he was visited by a young chief w a high rank and his wife, and they exchanged presents with Captain Cook. Summarily, Cook's visit to the islands was met with the utmost respect, most likely out of a perception of divinity, and the people allowed him to collect fresh water, restock on provisions, and trade. This introduced melon, pumpkin, and onion seeds to the shores of Hawaiʻi, and his entire crew were, on the whole, treated very hospitably by the natives.

A drawing of a heiau at Waimea, Kauaʻi, that was done by John Webber, a member of James Cook's expedition, circa 1778-1779. Engraved by D. K. Bonatti, after drawings by G. Gattina.
https://commons.wikimedia.org/wiki/File:Heiau_at_Waimea_by_John_Webber.jpg

Return Trip

By all accounts, Native Hawaiians were quite perplexed by the character and appearance of their new visitors and held them in high regard and wonder. The majority of natives saw Captain Cook as an incarnation of the god Lono, who, as the natives and priests had previously foretold and supposed, had returned in a different form to fulfill ancient prophecies. They rightly suspected that Cook and his crew had come from Kahiki and the other mysterious lands to the south of Hawaiʻi. Oral descriptions of Cook and his men were sent to Oʻahu, Maui, and the other islands by messengers.

The messengers said that "these men are white, their skin is loose and wrinkled, their heads are angular and from their mouths they breathe smoke and fire. Their bodies have openings into which they thrust their hands and bring out beads, nails, pieces of iron and other treasures. Their speech is unintelligible."

Captain Cook's second visit to Hawai'i came in the year 1779 after exploring the coast of Alaska and the Bering Strait and charting regions of the Arctic Ocean. Indeed, James Cook was a spectacular navigator and cartographer. Cook spent a few weeks sailing around the islands of Hawai'i, eventually anchoring in Kealakekua Bay. Records tell of an elderly priest venerating Cook's return with royal symbols of red feathered cloaks and valuable offerings. Upon landing, Cook was conducted to a *heiau* dedicated to the god Lono, where he was subjected to various ceremonies, and an image of him was installed as an incarnation of the god. Afterward, he was followed by priests and met with veneration and worship wherever he went, as priests would follow him with wands and advise the locals to prostrate themselves.

Around this time, the king of Hawai'i, Kalani'opu'u, was engaged in a war with a challenger for the throne, Kahekili. A few days after Cook's landing, King Kalani'opu'u made a grand visit to the ships of Captain Cook, bringing along three large canoes and bearing gifts of wickerwork idols that were adorned with jewelry. The idols were inlaid with mother of pearl and shark teeth. Captain Cook received the royal party on board the *Resolution* and presented the king with linen shirts and a handsome cutlass. Captain Cook also presented a firework show, which impressed the natives greatly, for they had never seen such things before.

Even so, the locals eventually began to tire of hosting Captain Cook and his men, as the newcomers were not aware of the local taboos and customs, which were called *kapu*. In fact, the Polynesian concept of *tapu* is where we derive our word "taboo" from. These violations by James Cook and his men would sow seeds of doubt about their supposedly divine nature, and the men were met with disgust. The lavish gifts also began to become burdensome and expensive, as meat and fresh produce were luxuries that were labor-intensive to procure. The death of one of the European sailors had also further disillusioned the natives' view of the men as incarnations of gods. As a result, quarrels and disputes over trading and exchanges became more and more common, gradually escalating into thefts and small fights.

Early in February of 1779, King Kalani'opu'u presented Captain Cook with an immense number of vegetables, an entire herd of swine, and an extensive collection of clothing and barkcloth. Cook was astonished at the volume and magnitude of the present, which was probably intended as a farewell gift meant to send them off. Captain Cook departed shortly after the gift was presented to him, and he set his sights on the Leeward Islands in the Caribbean. Unfortunately, he was met with a violent gale, and the *Resolution* damaged her foremast, forcing them to return to Kealakekua Bay for repairs. What greeted them was "an ominous silence everywhere...with not a canoe in sight." A boat sent ashore brought back news to Captain Cook that King Kalani'opu'u was absent and had placed the bay under *kapu*, effectively making the bay forbidden. Canoes with provisions were supplied, but the friendly manner that was previously expressed was nowhere to be found, and iron daggers were demanded in return for the provisions.

Shortly after, matters worsened, as a few natives stole some metal implements from the *Discovery*, either in retaliation for a perceived slight or for want of iron and metal. Palea, a chief who had been tasked with overseeing the people, went after the thieves, and a fight broke out between the natives and sailors that soured relations even more. That following night, a large and fast boat of the *Discovery* was stolen by the natives and broken up for the iron that held it together.

This caused Captain Cook to try and kidnap King Kalaniʻopuʻu and hold him prisoner until the stolen boat was returned. Such a tactic had worked for Cook before on other islands in the south. Thus, he went ashore with a lieutenant and nine sailors and headed toward Kalaniʻopuʻu's house. Cook's plan was to invite him to come aboard the *Resolution* and spend the day with him. Captain Cook's men had also formed a blockade of the bay with three boats that were well-armed and manned. Unfortunately, while Captain Cook was trying to invite King Kalaniʻopuʻu onto the *Resolution*, a canoe that knew nothing of the blockade came into the bay and was fired upon. Kalimu, the brother to Chief Palea, was killed, and news of his death was quickly sent to the king and his guards.

As a large crowd of armed natives gathered to bar Captain Cook's way back onto his ship, the king slowly realized that Captain Cook was his enemy. Captain Cook and his men tried to launch their boats and flee, but a fight ensued. Rocks, daggers, and swords were thrown, which resulted in Captain Cook being stabbed to death and four other sailors dying. Lieutenant John Gore, who was on board the *Resolution*, saw what was happening with his spyglass and ordered several cannon rounds to be shot into the crowd that was chasing the fleeing men. The aftermath saw seventeen natives killed. Captain Cook's body was taken to a *heiau*, and funerary rites were performed. His flesh was removed to be burned, and his bones were cleaned and deified. Eventually, some of his remains were taken by friendly priests to be given back to the sailors.

The Captain Cook memorial site, which says "Near This Spot Capt. James Cook Met His Death February 14 1779."
gillfoto, CC BY-SA 4.0 <https://creativecommons.org/licenses/by-sa/4.0>, via Wikimedia Commons https://commons.wikimedia.org/wiki/File:Hawaii_WikiC_9015.jpg

Even after his death, the journals and writings of James Cook brought many other explorers and sailors to the islands of Hawaiʻi, forever changing the lives of Native Hawaiians. Cook's unexpected death dissuaded other expeditions toward the Hawaiian Islands for over seven years, and in this time, Hawaiʻi was separated into three smaller kingdoms following the breakup of Kalaniʻopuʻu's kingdom. Around the year 1780, Kalaniʻopuʻu held a great council among his high chiefs to settle the succession of his kingdom, and among those present was Kalaniʻopuʻu's nephew, Kamehameha. Kamehameha was appointed the religious leader and representative of the Hawaiian god of war, Ku-kaʻili-moku. King Kalaniʻopuʻu died in the spring of 1782, and the redistribution of lands was customary after the passing of a *moʻi*, or great ruler. Chaos and power struggles followed his passing, and many fights and rebellions followed in the years to come.

More to Come

Part of the narrative of Captain Cook's last voyages showed the potential profits that could be made by trading and exploration. Fur traders reaped in profits from trading with the Native Americans of the northwest coast of America. Expeditions from India, England, China, and various parts of the Americas set out to engage in this trade, with the main rendezvous point being Vancouver Island. The island was located just above what is now the northern border between the United States of America and Canada. The small body of water that lay on the western edge of Vancouver Island was called Nootka Sound, with "sound" meaning a part of the sea that turns into an inlet of sorts.

The first recorded ships that visited the Hawaiian Islands after the death of James Cook were the *King George*, which was commanded by Captain Nathaniel Portlock, and the *Queen Charlotte*, which was commanded by Captain George Dixon. Both of these commanders had served under Captain Cook before and set off from London to sail together. They were not welcome at Kealakekua Bay and went toward Oʻahu instead, anchoring themselves in Waiʻalae Bay. Around the same time, a French explorer reached the eastern shores of Maui near Honuaʻula. Dixon and Portlock bought food and fresh water with iron nails and metal weapons. Captain Portlock also noted that almost all of the iron daggers that were sold, traded, and gifted by Captain Cook had ended up in the hands of Kahekili and his warriors. A few months later, Dixon and Portlock visited the islands of Hawaiʻi again in 1786, trading hoops of iron, beads, and nails for provisions, wood, and water. They made land at Waiʻalae, Oʻahu, and Waimea, Kauaʻi, before moving on toward China.

One of the notable visits to Kauaʻi was the *Nootka*, a ship that was led by Captain John Meares. After spending a month at Kauaʻi, a famous chief named Kaʻiana went with Captain Meares as a passenger, where they continued toward Canton, China, now known as modern-day Guangzhou. Kaʻiana was known to Captain Portlock as Tyanna, an Anglicized form of the Hawaiian pronunciation, and he was a tall man. Kaʻiana was a guest of his English friends and had a warm and hospitable stay. Because of his tall stature and his feathered cape and helmet, Kaʻiana would walk the streets of Canton and terrify the local Chinese people with his imposing figure.

After three months, Captain Meares outfitted and commissioned two vessels, the *Felice Adventurer* and *Iphigenia*, to further carry out fur trades and take Kaʻiana and three other natives as passengers. Kaʻiana boarded *Iphigenia*, which was commanded by Captain William Douglas, and Kaʻiana arrived back on the island of Hawaiʻi at Kealakekua Bay, where he was greeted by Kamehameha. The welcoming party consisted of twelve large double canoes that were beautifully decorated and adorned. Unfortunately, Kamehameha brought news that Kaʻeo, the king of Kauaʻi, had turned hostile toward Kaʻiana, and Kaʻiana accepted

Kamehameha's offer to enter into his service as a form of protection. At this time, the Hawaiian Islands were plagued by warfare and instability, and Kamehameha recognized the advantage of having a chief who was learned and familiar with foreign ways on his side. Kaʻiana was granted a large property to live on and oversee as his own territory on the island of Hawaiʻi. In return, Kaʻiana's collection of foreign goods, tools, and firearms was now under the indirect control of Kamehameha.

Kamehameha Rising

Shortly after landing on the island of Hawaiʻi, Kaʻiana asked Captain Douglas to gift Kamehameha a swivel cannon to be mounted on a large double canoe. After much persuasion, Captain Douglas relented. This was one of the first recorded instances of Kamehameha compiling firearms and gathering his military strength.

King Kamehameha I depicted at spear practice.
https://commons.wikimedia.org/wiki/File:Kamehameha_I_at_Spear_Practice_(1),_from_Brother_Bertram_Photograph_Collection.jpg

In particular, a high chief and counselor to Kamehameha named Kameʻeiamoku ambushed an American ship, the *Fair American*, in retaliation for earlier offenses by another American vessel, the *Eleanor*, which was captained by Simon Metcalfe. Captain Metcalfe had also used the *Eleanor* to massacre over one hundred innocent natives at Olowalu, Maui, in 1790 because Olowalu was the home village of the suspected thieves of one of Captain Metcalfe's boats. This incident would go on to be known as the Olowalu Massacre. By coincidence, the *Fair*

American was captained by Simon Metcalfe's son, Thomas Metcalfe.

The *Fair American* was seized, and Thomas Metcalfe was killed, along with almost all of the crew. The only survivor was Isaac Davis, who was a mate aboard the ship, and he was rounded up with John Young, a detained boatswain who was previously aboard the *Eleanora*. These two would be treated with kindness and generosity by Kameʻeiamoku because Kamehameha wanted them on his side for their expertise in handling muskets and cannons. They were raised to the rank of chief and paid for their services in war and their counsel. Troops of men were trained by Young and Davis in musketry and shooting, and in time, they would prove to be invaluable advisors and generals for King Kamehameha.

Thereafter, Kamehameha sent a summons to Keoua Kuʻahuʻula, a son of the former King Kalaniʻopuʻu, and Keawemaʻuhili, who was the half-brother to King Kalaniʻopuʻu, making him Kamehameha's uncle, for more men and canoes. Keoua Kuʻahuʻula refused, but Kamehameha was backed by his uncle Keawemaʻuhili, who sent men along with his own sons.

With this, Kamehameha finally felt strong enough to invade and take over the island of Maui.

After consolidating a large force of men and canoes, Kamehameha crossed the channel in the summer of 1790 and landed in Hana and then Hamakualoa. Here, he defeated the vanguard of the Maui forces and moved his fleet to Kahului, where he eventually clashed with the Maui army, which was led by Kahekili's sons. The two field artillery squads that were led by Young and Davis, along with Kamehameha's significant advantage in musketry and firepower, pushed the Maui warriors back and broke their morale. Kamehameha was victorious and showed no mercy to the vanquished factions, driving them over cliffs and forcing them to barricade themselves in crags and caves, where they were starved out.

However, Kamehameha's conquest of Maui was not permanent. Due to his absence on the island of Hawaiʻi, Keoua Kuʻahuʻula invaded the district of Hilo and killed Keawemaʻuhili. Upon hearing this news, Kamehameha sailed back with all of his forces from Molokaʻi to Hawaiʻi, landing at Kawaihae. The resulting battles pushed Keoua Kuʻahuʻula back and forced a retreat, but the battles were indecisive.

Kamehameha fell back to Waipi'o to recover from his losses, while Keoua Ku'ahu'ula fell back to Hilo, where he began planning his next move. Finally, in November 1790, Keoua Ku'ahu'ula set out on an overland route that passed by the volcano Kilauea. He and his forces made camp there for two days, even though the crater was showing signs of activity. As luck would have it, Kilauea erupted on the third day, spewing noxious clouds of black sand, hot cinder, and bits of lava. The terrific earthquake and destructive shower killed more than half of Keoua Ku'ahu'ula's men and forced him to move before he was ready. Kamehameha saw the eruption as a divine sign from the goddess Pele that he was the rightful heir of Hawai'i.

A year later, in 1791, Kamehameha finally captured and killed Keoua Ku'ahu'ula, who had all but given up the struggle. Kamehameha had Keoua and some of his warriors sacrificed to the god of war, Ku-ka'ili-moku, at the Pu'ukohola Heiau. This made Kamehameha the undisputed master of the island of Hawai'i.

Ruins of the Pu'ukohola Heiau. Image taken in 2007.
Bamse, CC BY-SA 4.0 <https://creativecommons.org/licenses/by-sa/4.0>, via Wikimedia Commons https://commons.wikimedia.org/wiki/File:Pu%27ukohola_Heiau_temple2.jpg

Kahekili would pass away in July of 1794, making his descendants, relatives, and other chiefs fight and quarrel over matters in his absence. Subsequently, his kingdom would fall into chaos, and since it was so spread out and disunited, the lands all fell one by one to Kamehameha. In

1795, due to infighting between Kahekili's eldest son, Kalanikupule, and other family members, Kamehameha saw that the time had now come to conquer the other islands. Mustering up all his arms and men, Kamehameha commanded what was probably the largest and best-equipped army that the Hawaiian archipelago had seen at that time. Kamehameha's war party would sail to Lahaina, Maui, and raze the west coast. The commanding chief, Koalaukane, had fled to Oʻahu without putting up any resistance. Kamehameha would then move on Molokaʻi. His battle with the troops on Oʻahu would be fierce, but Kamehameha would prevail, making him master of all the islands except Kauaʻi and Niʻihau.

Before launching his attack on Kauaʻi and Niʻihau, Kamehameha employed foreign mechanics to build him a massive vessel that weighed forty tons and was armed with many four-pound cannons. In spite of his plans, Kamehameha did not wait to complete this ship before sailing for war on Kauaʻi. He had dedicated and consecrated a *heiau* in Ewa with human sacrifices and moved his army and fleet to Waiʻanae. From there, they sailed under cover of night to Kauaʻi, but the fleet encountered a fierce tempest that wrecked many of his canoes and forced them back to Waiʻanae.

During this time, Kamehameha was also facing a rebellion against his authority back on the island of Hawaiʻi. This caused him to sail back to Hawaiʻi with the bulk of his forces and crush the rising rebellion. This was the last of Kamehameha's wars, and it put to rest any other thoughts of challenging his rule. Since the island of Niʻihau did not possess many resources or opposition,

Kamehameha ignored it and eventually negotiated a peaceful unification between the lands he ruled with the island of Kaua'i. He cemented his position as the first king of a united Hawai'i, which would be called the Kingdom of Hawai'i.

Statue of King Kamehameha I in the hall of the United States Capitol.
Alacoolwiki, CC BY-SA 4.0 <https://creativecommons.org/licenses/by-sa/4.0>, via Wikimedia Commons https://commons.wikimedia.org/wiki/File:Kamehameha_Ier_2.jpg

Chapter 5 – The Kingdom of Hawai'i

Although the concept of land ownership is markedly different for Native Hawaiians than Europeans, for example, it is still accurate to say that the history of Hawaiian lands is a history of those lands moving from the hands of Native Hawaiian people into the hands of others.

Different Systems of Tenure

A successive chain of Native Hawaiian monarchs tried valiantly to retain their sovereignty over the lands of Hawai'i, but they were ultimately unsuccessful. This pattern of political development is not atypical; almost every other group of islands in the Pacific also fell to Western rule over the course of a few hundred years. For example, de facto control over New Zealand was slowly given over to Great Britain, first through a treaty signed by Māori chiefs in 1840 and then by the chiefs of Fiji, who transferred sovereignty over to Queen Victoria in 1874. Great Britain would go on to claim Tuvalu and Kiribati, followed by the southern Solomon Islands, as their territories or protectorates.

Before European influence and political maneuvers, the prevailing system of land ownership was a native-centric arrangement that was complex and based on interdependent agricultural and societal needs. This was expressed in a spirit of reciprocity between the people and the land, or *'aina*. *'Aina* was not something that could be traded, sold, or bought. It is more accurate to say that the land was to be controlled through a system of joint responsibility and accountability that was to be managed by the chiefs of Hawai'i, the *ali'i*. The Hawaiian system of land tenure perceived any handling of land in a transactional manner to be debasing to both one's family and themselves. As such, even the chiefs and kings were only to deal with land distribution and portioning merely as trustees of a higher authority.

Death by Disease

Tragically, the foreigners to Hawai'i brought many germs, pathogens, and viruses that infected the local native population. The islands of Hawai'i had long been isolated from the rest of the world with little to no contact with emerging pathogens. This meant that the people of Hawai'i were very susceptible and vulnerable to these foreign diseases. Further worsening the problem was the tight social connections and communal lifestyles that were the cultural norm of the Hawaiians, leading to fast-spreading outbreaks.

Additionally, there was a marked scarcity in the supply of doctors, and epidemics ravaged the Native Hawaiians in waves. By the 1800s, the native population had been utterly devastated. Venereal diseases such as gonorrhea and syphilis ran rampant due to no effective treatment being available at the time. It is suspected that these viruses and infections, which were colloquially given the nickname of the "Curse of Cook," were a major factor in the drastic drop of the Native Hawaiians' birthrate. Moreover, sicknesses like tuberculosis, leprosy, and scabies made life very uncomfortable, painful, and scary. Dysentery, cholera, and typhoid fever further served to weaken the population, so much so that sudden deaths were commonplace. Family members might go a few days without seeing another relative, only to realize they had passed away while working, gathering food, or going about their daily activities. Local estimates put the number of deaths over the years as "cutting the population in half," which modern analysis confirms.

Hawaiians lacked the immunities that were adapted via exposure that many of their Western visitors and guests had, meaning they succumbed to the common cold and flu at a much higher rate. Measles and mumps outbreaks also occurred and resulted in childhood deaths and further population decline. In the 1850s, despite the best preventive efforts of visiting captains, traders, and merchants, a smallpox outbreak infected well over six thousand Hawaiians and resulted in thousands of deaths.

Such a drastic and irreparable decline in native peoples, combined with the slow and steady influx of foreigners and their culture, caused an increasing state of disorder and confusion in the Kingdom of Hawai'i. As individuals died and their plots of land were abandoned, people from rural communities slowly began to leave and move closer to the expanding urban centers. Trading, medicine, and social support were more readily available in the more densely populated places. The more isolated villages and farms were neglected and abandoned, as the amount of manpower a community or family had slowly decreased and, with it, their capacity for farming and supporting themselves.

Changing Religions

The palpable desperation that permeated Hawai'i because of the consecutive waves of epidemics caused a significant change in the religious composition of the islands. People who sought treatment and answers from their traditional priests and shamans were not satisfied with what they received. Hawaiians relied on their spiritual heritage and depended on their healers and leaders to show them a way to survive these troubled times. Additionally, old-standing religious beliefs would be challenged by the arrival and proselytization of Christian missionaries. Many Native Hawaiians converted to Christianity, mostly either as entire families or as individuals who did not have anywhere else to go.

An artist's depiction of the Ahu'ena Heiau in 1816.
https://commons.wikimedia.org/wiki/File:Ahuena_heiau_1816.jpg

Another big factor in the gradual discontinuation of the old ways was the effect of two leading female *ali'i*, who challenged the status quo and the status of *kapu*. These two individuals were Ka'ahumanu and Keopuolani, both of whom were wives of King Kamehameha I. Polygamy was more common for Hawaiian royalty than it was for normal Hawaiians, with high-ranking chiefs and kings having multiple wives. Ka'ahumanu and Keopuolani were politically powerful and saw the *kapu* system as oppressive to women, and they detested it. They pushed harder to abolish the system after King Kamehameha I's death, and Kamehameha II, who was the son of King Kamehameha I, decided to support his mother and end numerous *kapu* practices. These included the end of various task segregations by sex and also implicitly allowed more of the missionary-led destruction of many temples and idols of the islands to occur. This extraordinary event was a landmark moment, for "the Hawai'i of old" was no more. Historians and scholars today also strongly believe that the move to abolish these old systems also allowed the Kamehameha dynasty to further protect their political supremacy by ensuring other chiefs no longer had access to the traditional ways of gaining or claiming rank, prestige, or sociocultural approval.

Queen Kaʻahumanu with her servant, a painting by Louis Choris, 1816.
https://commons.wikimedia.org/wiki/File:Kaahumanu_with_servant.jpg

This "spiritual power vacuum" was promptly filled by Protestant missionaries, especially once a group of Calvinists that hailed from the American Board of Commissioners for Foreign Missions got permission from King Kamehameha II to stay on the islands. These missionaries soon set out for Oʻahu and Kauaʻi, and they slowly gained followers and political power. They accomplished this very effectively by establishing schools and teaching the English language and system of writing. These new opportunities for employment, housing, learning, and a place of belonging attracted many Native Hawaiians to the newcomers. The missionaries also claimed that the reason the diseases ravaged the islanders so brutally was their failure to believe in Jesus Christ and his divine message. Eventually, Queen Keopuolani became the first *aliʻi* to officially convert to Christianity in 1823.

The Tragic Trip

In an effort to thank King George IV for the gift of a gunship, King Kamehameha II traveled to London aboard the British whaling ship *L'Aigle* in 1823. He also intended for the trip to foster closer diplomatic ties between his budding kingdom and the British. On the way, the ship arrived at Rio de Janeiro to visit the newly independent Empire of Brazil and exchange luxurious gifts with Emperor Pedro I. Unbeknownst to both parties, both the Empire of Brazil and the Kingdom of Hawaiʻi would eventually fall. Nonetheless, King Kamehameha II and his wife, Queen Kamamalu, arrived in Portsmouth six months after they had set sail from Hawaiʻi. They were moved into the Caledonian Hotel in London and greeted hospitably by members of the British government. However, the local press treated their arrival with confusion and ridicule, misspelling King Kamehameha II's birthname (Liholiho) name and making fun of the Hawaiian Islands.

Rhio Rhio, King of the Sandwich Islands, a sketch done in London by an unknown artist with a misspelling of Liholiho's name.
https://commons.wikimedia.org/wiki/File:Kamehameha_II_in_London.jpg

Regardless, King Kamehameha II and his entourage toured London and were well looked after by their hosts. They visited Westminster Abbey, attended ballet and opera shows at the Royal Opera House and the Theatre Royal, and also had portraits made of them. King Kamehameha II was said to be quite a sight for the British people, as he was over six feet tall, well-built, and dark-skinned. Unfortunately, both King Kamehameha II and his queen contracted measles and had no immunity to the disease. Queen Kamamalu died on July 8th, 1824, and her grief-stricken husband passed away six days later on July 14th. Their bodies were kept in the crypt of an Anglican church and later returned back to Hawai'i aboard the Royal Navy frigate the HMS *Blonde*. King Kamehameha II's brother, Kauikeaouli, succeeded the throne of the Kingdom of Hawai'i and became King Kamehameha III.

The Continuation of the Kingdom

The untimely death of King Kamehameha II and his queen in London only served to solidify the powers and influence of missionaries in Hawaiian society. This was further demonstrated when the procession of King Kamehameha II's body was led with Anglican prayers, including similar prayers said in the Hawaiian language. Before his departure, King Kamehameha II had named his brother to be the ruler in his absence, but since Kauikeaouli was only nine years old, Ka'ahumanu, the wife of King Kamehameha I, assumed control of the Kingdom of Hawai'i. She shared power with another high chief named Kalanimoku, who was her cousin. Kalanimoku was also known as Karaimoku and reputedly had great political and business acumen. This earned him the nickname "the Iron Cable of Hawai'i."

Kauikeaouli, or King Kamehameha III, would come to power after the death of Ka'ahumanu, which happened when he was eighteen years old. He inherited all of the former problems of his predecessors. His subjects continued to suffer immensely from disease epidemics, and foreigners continued to badger and demand more goods and produce from the islands, along with allotments of land. Interestingly, King Kamehameha III decided to embrace older cultural traditions and worked to secure his kingdom against foreign interests for the good of his people. His upbringing saw him torn between the Christian teachings of Kaʻahumanu and the old Hawaiian traditions. He was influenced by a young Hawaiian-Tahitian priest named Kaomi, with whom King Kamehameha III was also intimate. Intimate same-sex relationships, *moe aikane*, were common among Hawaiian royalty and were accepted as normal and natural by Hawaiians for hundreds of years. This relationship earned Kamehameha III the anger and disapproval of the Christian missionaries.

A portrait of King Kamehameha III.
https://commons.wikimedia.org/wiki/File:Kamehameha_III.jpg

King Kamehameha III worked to reinvigorate the cultural traditions of his people, and he encouraged them to partake in precolonial pastimes like hula, games, kava drinking, and other practices that were discouraged and forbidden by the Christian missionaries. This caused some amount of strife between *aliʻi* that were Christian and other chiefs who were not. King Kamehameha III would try to ease tensions and bridge the divide by providing younger chiefs and *aliʻi* with formal Western schooling and language lessons. Through this, King Kamehameha III hoped to increase their flexibility and mediating ability when it came to complex issues that involved both Hawaiian and Westernized parts of society. He asked the American Missionary Society for a teacher to educate royal children, and they provided a teacher and his wife, which led to the establishment of a special school in Hawaiʻi for children of royal lineage.

King Kamehameha III also encoded many laws into actual text-based legislation. This was one of his most important contributions, as he helped codify the native rights of the Hawaiian people, especially the *makaʻainana*. Despite that, foreigners began increasingly demanding land, whether through their businesses or through economically-driven political interests. As the number of foreigners arriving on the Hawaiian Islands increased, so did the pressure on Hawaiian rulers and leaders to grant them some form of land ownership, whether to protect foreign capital investments or to provide new job opportunities for local Hawaiians.

This eventually drove King Kamehameha III to make the Declaration of Rights of 1839, which was followed very closely by the Constitution of 1840. Both of these are incredibly important documents in the history of Hawaiʻi. These documents were designed to protect the interests of all inhabitants of the kingdom and made drastic changes to the authority of the chiefs and head chiefs. These documents prohibited the oppression of the *makaʻainana* and stipulated that any chief or head chief who violated its laws must be removed from their position of power. The Declaration of Rights states that "it is not proper to enact laws that protect and enrich the rulers only, without regard to the enriching of their subjects also." Centrally, the Declaration put forth property rights for the people of Hawai'i, securing their lands for them. It states that as long as they conformed to the laws of the Kingdom of Hawai'i, nothing may be taken from them.

These documents were notable because they were not passed under duress or by an unwilling sovereign. Instead, it was a wise decision by a prudent ruler. King Kamehameha III understood the new wave of logic, needs, and principles that were being brought forth by Western norms, and the passing of these documents clearly heralded a new age in the civilization of his kingdom. Further, the 1840 Constitution explains the very concept of traditional Hawaiian thought as it pertains to land ownership, stating that although the land had belonged to King Kamehameha I, it was not his private property. He was merely the head of the management of that landed property. Such explicit acknowledgment of the relationship between the *ali'i*, the *maka'ainana*, and the lands of Hawai'i by this constitution was an important milestone in Native Hawaiian rights.

Sadly, representatives of foreign powers continued insisting on lands to lease and rent. These major foreign powers, namely the United States, Great Britain, and France, disguised their requests and demands as concerns over their citizens not being able to secure the future of their capital investments and to lease land for a fee. At times, these demands would be supported by the presence of warships. Spurred on by visits from the French and the Americans, an admiral of the Royal Navy, Lord George Paulet, sailed his warship to Honolulu in 1843 and made several demands under threat of violence and force. These demands included debt payments and legal rights for British subjects. The Hawaiian government was forced to accede to his demands, and King

Kamehameha III signed an agreement stating as such. Paulet then destroyed every Hawaiian flag he could find and raised the British Union Flag during his period of occupation. Approximately five months later, the land would be surrendered back to the Kingdom of Hawai'i by British Rear Admiral Richard Thomas, who negotiated financial settlements and resolved the disputes of sovereignty over the land.

A picture of George Paulet, who was promoted to rear admiral on July 21", 1856.
https://commons.wikimedia.org/wiki/File:George_Paulet_(Royal_Navy_officer).jpg

This was clearly worrisome for the future of the Kingdom of Hawai'i, and it caused King

Kamehameha III great distress. With the instability of political and military powers in the Hawaiian archipelago, he consulted his foreign advisors and missionaries on what he should do to protect the kingdom's sovereignty and ensure Hawaiian control of the land. Clearly, foreign powers wanted Hawai'i's system of land tenure to transition to one of private ownership for their own benefit, as they were familiar with such a system and wanted to obtain secure land titles. They further promoted such changes by pointing out that it would be a great help in steering the islands toward economic prosperity and encourage hard work. Predictably, large numbers of Hawaiian natives were deeply suspicious of the proposed changes and continually petitioned King Kamehameha III to reconsider his position on the matter. The local chiefs and residents were hesitant to compete with foreigners, as the change to the land tenure system would be confusing and difficult. Regardless, the Land Commission and King Kamehameha III proceeded with the Mahele process.

The Great Mahele

As the great foreign powers of Great Britain, the United States, and France vied over the muchcoveted lands and ports of Hawai'i and other territories in the Pacific region, Hawai'i experienced increasing political, military, and economic pressure from all sides. In line with many of his foreign advisors' counsel, King Kamehameha III realized that he had to assuage the demands for land from the Westerners, especially the ones who were already living in the Kingdom of Hawai'i.

King Kamehameha III was greatly beloved by his people and was considered to be one of Hawai'i's greatest rulers. This was partly because he stood astride both Western and Hawaiian cultures, being raised with Christian teachings and having learned the ways of Western politics. He was learned in English but simultaneously focused on promoting and giving his people back their old traditions and cultural identity. Historians note that he ensured no laws enforced any class distinctions and that he also carried forward the annulment of the *kapu* system that his mother had started during her period as queen regent.

In 1845, King Kamehameha III approved of the creation of a complex governmental group that is usually referred to as the Land Commission. This group consisted of a number of native and foreign lawyers, chiefs, businessmen, and legislators. They were in charge of overseeing land claims and disputes. Over time, it came to pass that there was to be a Great Division, also known as the Great Mahele, which was intended to be an overarching legal restructuring of the lands of Hawai'i and their tenure system. King Kamehameha III would retain his own lands, and he would divide the remainder of lands into thirds that would be given to the government, the *ali'i* (chiefs), and the *maka'ainana* (common people). King Kamehameha III's own land claims would be subject to dispute and residential claims, but most of the king's lands were not contested. Many *ali'i* relinquished certain parts of their lands or interests to King Kamehameha III, and the king did the same with respect to the plots of land that the *ali'i* wanted.

In 1848, the divisional claims were completed, and King Kamehameha III held titles to almost 2.5 million acres of land, which amounted to around 60 percent of the Kingdom of Hawai'i.

However, King Kamehameha III ceded about 1.5 million acres to the government in order to satisfy demands and alleviate the economic and political burdens of his people. These 1.5 million acres came to be known as the "Government Lands" and were, in theory, also subject to the disputes and counterclaims of the *maka'ainana*. Summarily, the ruler held about 24 percent of the land, the government held about 37 percent of the land, and the remaining 39 percent was allotted to the *ali'i*. The underlying idea was for the *ali'i* to give up roughly half of the lands that they had titles for to the *maka'ainana* and the remainder to be made up through disputes, claims, and donations.

Unfortunately, the people of Hawai'i came to possess very little land in the end. They ended up being the clear losers over the course of the Great Mahele. Many of the *ali'i* ended up selling off their lands and land titles, whether by choice or by force. Subsequently, many of the *maka'ainana* who were reliant on the land rights of their *ali'i* were left homeless and lost their native tenancies. Many of the common people were confused and uninformed about what to do to obtain their land. They still largely believed in and operated by the traditional notion of land ownership, thinking they always had access to whatever lands they needed to survive and live. In fact, many preferred the old system and refused to change. Due to this friction, the government met to discuss the shortcomings of the Mahele process and adopted four resolutions that would be collectively known as the Kuleana Act of 1850. This act encouraged the *maka'ainana* to file claims with the Land Commission and extended the deadline. Still, these supplementary policies and reforms did not end up benefiting the people of Hawai'i much. Filing claims was a tedious and long process that was not explained to the Hawaiian masses. Furthermore, a claim could only be filed after a survey had been arranged and paid for, along with two witnesses to validate the entire thing. This cost money that a lot of people did not have, and reports from this time note an utter lack of qualified surveyors in the Kingdom of Hawai'i. As a result, the claims and surveys often became a matter of bribery and fraud, with many instances of favoritism, intentional delays, inconsistencies, and conflicts of interest. The Land Commission also did not establish clear rules or regulations to help smooth the process along, and many claims were rejected or left incomplete.

In total, over 14,000 claims were filed, but only about 8,400 were approved, which means roughly only 30 percent of the Native Hawaiians gained titles and rights. The average amount of land granted was about three acres, which meant that out of the millions of acres that were supposed to be distributed amongst the people of Hawai'i, less than twenty-nine thousand acres were actually given out. In other words, the Native Hawaiian commoners owned approximately

1 percent of Hawai'i's land area. The total amount that was owned was small enough to fit on the island of Kaho'olawe. By comparison, thirty-three missionary families had obtained roughly forty-one thousand acres of land.

Chapter 6 – The United States and Hawai'i

Any history of Hawai'i would be woefully incomplete without the inclusion of a specific chapter dedicated to the long history and relationship between the United States of America and Hawai'i. The effect of American culture on Hawai'i was so marked that from the 1800s onward, most cities and major towns of Hawai'i looked more American.

The streets were lined with churches, schools, commercial buildings, and residences that were fashioned after Western architecture and layouts. The language, music, and laws of Hawai'i were Americanized, sporting only hints and influences of native culture. Indisputably, Hawai'i was the subject of marketing, with ads touting a tropical and exotic paradise that also happened to have bottled beer, billiard tables, and tracks for horse cars.

Much of these influences can be attributed to the arrival of Christian missionaries, with most sources agreeing that this began with the arrival of seventeen Protestant missionaries in 1820. Like most Christian missionary writings of first contact with native peoples all over the world, the Hawaiian people were regarded and described by the Protestant missionaries as "dirty, lazy, spiritually ignorant and wild" people. Such a description was plainly false, as Native Hawaiians were decidedly industrious, especially from an exploratory and agricultural perspective. They had deep spiritual roots and had extensive cultural and social norms, which were all built around an extended unit of the family.

A mission school in Lahaina, Maui, 1909.
Internet Archive Book Images, No restrictions, via Wikimedia Commons
https://commons.wikimedia.org/wiki/File:Mission_school_children,_Lahaina,_Maui,_Hawaii(14594885519).jpg

Nonetheless, there is strong evidence that points to the fact that Hawai'i is unmistakably American in feeling and action. Perhaps the largest objections to such claims are the historical track record of maltreatment of Native Hawaiians by foreigners and Americans, as well as the huge population of Japanese people living on the islands. The second point was a sore subject in the eyes of mainland Americans when schools kept the Japanese language. Japan also launched propaganda aimed at sowing discord amongst the Americans.

Western Influence

Hawai'i was no stranger to Western political agendas, which were inflicted onto many island nations in the Pacific. In reality, many powers tried to wrest control of the Hawaiian Islands from the natives. Very early on, in 1794, Captain George Vancouver (after whom the city of Vancouver is named) claimed the islands for Great Britain and hoisted its flag on several of the islands. However, his reports and actions were not ratified by London in time to be of any practical use. Furthermore, the Russians had also staked a claim over the islands of Hawai'i. The governor of Alaska at that time sent a vessel to Honolulu, ordering the construction of buildings that were fitted with mounted guns. They, too, hoisted the Russian flag over these buildings. Fortunately, King Kamehameha I built a large fort in Honolulu and expelled the Russians, eventually causing the Russian government to disavow their Russian agents. As the decades passed, the English residents of Hawai'i did not approve of or enjoy the American occupation of the islands. They frequently demanded meetings and consultations with American officials. The American presence was bolstered by the USS *Mohican*, a steampowered warship that was originally assigned to the Pacific Squadron but was later assigned to patrol and reinforce Hawai'i in the late 1880s.

The French also threatened war with King Kamehameha III in 1839 if the king did not relax the laws restricting the activities of French Catholic missionaries. Once the French had taken over the Marquesas Islands and established their own protectorate over Tahiti, they set their sights on the islands of Hawai'i and began disputing the claims of the British residents and officers of the Hawaiian Islands. This eventually led to a British show of force with warships, which caused King Kamehameha III to cede the sovereignty of the Kingdom of Hawai'i to Great Britain in 1843. Interestingly, this action was reversed by British Rear Admiral Richard Thomas when he, based on his understanding of British foreign policy, took down the British flag and proclaimed the sovereignty of the Hawaiian Islands back under the control of the king of Hawai'i. Other military incursions continued throughout the years. One other instance involved French sailors landing and destroying large parts of the Honolulu fort in 1849.

The Decline of the Kingdom of Hawai'i

King Kamehameha III died not too long after the Great Mahele, on December 14th, 1854. This led to disputes over who should inherit his lands and titles. Eventually, matters were settled in accordance with King Kamehameha III's wishes, and his adopted son, Alexander Liholiho (not to be confused with King Kamehameha II, whose birth name was Liholiho), was to become the successor to the throne. He was proclaimed King Kamehameha IV by his biological father, Mataio Kekuanao'a, who was the governor of O'ahu. Tragically, King Kamehameha IV's rule was cut short by his unexpected and premature passing. His rule lasted only nine years.

Frontal portrait of King Kamehameha IV, Alexander Liholiho.
https://commons.wikimedia.org/wiki/File:Kamehameha_IV,_lithograph_by_Grozelier_(cropped).jpg

He had suffered from chronic asthma for quite some time and was also deeply in grief over the death of his four-year-old son, Prince Albert, in 1862. These events proved to be too great for Alexander Liholiho; he passed away at the young age of twenty-nine. Then, a council consisting of the members of the Hawaiian Cabinet and other advisors to the king decided that because there was no heir to the throne, Prince Lot Kapuaiwa, the older brother of the late King Kamehameha IV, was to become king. He would go on to become King Kamehameha V. However, because of Alexander Liholiho's sudden death and lack of political preparation, many factions did not see Prince Lot's ascension as legitimate, especially since there was no joint ballot undertaken with the House of Nobles and the House of Representatives, which were major players in Hawai'i's political sphere. In spite of these objections, Victoria Kamamalu, sister to both Prince Lot and Alexander Liholiho, was rightly instituted as the queen regent (*Kuhina Nui*). And under Article 47 of the 1852 Constitution of the Kingdom of Hawai'i, she was well within her powers to name a successor to the throne in the absence of the king. She named Lot.

In a strange course of fate, King Kamehameha V also reigned for only nine years, passing away on December 11th, 1872, at the age of forty-two. Yet again, a named successor was not available to ascend the throne, and this caused some amount of confusion and consternation. During this time, William Charles Lunalilo emerged as a favorite for the throne, as he had attended the Royal School, which was run by American missionaries. William Lunalilo was also a descendant of Kalaimamahu, who was the half-brother of King Kamehameha I. He was chosen by an overwhelming majority of a collection of male electorates and was soon confirmed as the successor to the throne by the legislature of Hawai'i. Again, as ill fate would have it, Lunalilo would become king, only to pass away a little over a year later due to complications of tuberculosis and other related ailments.

Nevertheless, during his short reign, King Lunalilo enacted laws that would change the course of Hawai'i's history forever. In a move that was considered very divisive, King Lunalilo offered to exchange the lagoon of Pearl Harbor to the United States in exchange for the exemption of taxes on a number of Hawaiian goods that were exported to the United States, mainly sugar. However, the king withdrew the offer before it was deemed official due to significant pushback from the other *ali'i* and the general public. This event showed that the people and rulers of Hawai'i harbored deep feelings of distrust, bitterness, and suspicion toward foreign involvement and land treaties. Additionally, King Lunalilo behaved contrary to King Kamehameha V's example by electing three American ministers to seats of power and by cooperating and associating himself with the missionaries.

After King Lunalilo's death in 1874, the updated Constitution of 1864 assigned the task of choosing an heir to the Cabinet Council along with the Legislative Assembly. The two main royals that were considered were Queen Emma, who was the widow of King Kamehameha IV, and David Kalakaua, a descendant of a high-ranking *ali'i* who hailed from Hilo. Both David Kalakaua and Queen Emma were passionately patriotic and wanted to help preserve the royal line and the Kingdom of Hawai'i. A divide between the foreign powers' support for each of these royals began to form, with British interests aligning more with Queen Emma and American interests aligning more with David Kalakaua. Eventually, the legislature elected David Kalakaua, and this ended the Kamehameha era of the Kingdom of Hawai'i.

King David Kalakaua, circa 1870s.
https://commons.wikimedia.org/wiki/File:Kalakaua_(PP-96-15-008).jpg

King Kalakaua's ascension to the throne started the Keawe-a-Heulu royal line and saw a time of growing American influence on the Hawaiian Islands. Even though David Kalakaua was advised against going forward with the Reciprocity Treaty, he negotiated with the Americans and eventually ratified the bill in 1875. This treaty essentially allowed free trade between Hawai'i and the United States, but more importantly, it did not sign over any Hawaiian land to the Americans. However, many legislators and businessmen suspected that this would give the United States economic leverage over Hawai'i and eventually lead to American annexation (an illegal administrative conquest backed by force) of the area of Pu'u Loa, which would later be called Pearl Harbor.

Afterward, foreign interests and plantation companies dearly wanted to invest more resources into the sugar plantations of Hawaiʻi and especially buy more land. However, they were barred from doing so. King Kamehameha V had passed an act in 1865 that prohibited any alienation of the crown lands. The economic boom was immense and pushed the Western-run press to consistently publish and promote propaganda and articles that were in favor of selling more land, stating that allowing such transactions to take place would benefit all, no matter their class. Many foreign investors, spokespeople, businessmen, and newspapers repeated the view that more sales of land would lead to an influx of revenue in Hawaiʻi and enable both the royal family and the nation at large to benefit and prosper, enjoying a more secure, modern, and higher quality of life.

Eight years into his reign as king, David Kalakaua would turn against the United States' interests and seek a more independent path for the Kingdom of Hawaiʻi. This move would ultimately lead to the Bayonet Constitution being forced on Kalakaua in 1887 and the overthrowing of the Kingdom of Hawaiʻi.

The Bayonet Constitution and the Overthrow of the Kingdom of Hawaiʻi

The Hawaiian kingdom effectively ended in 1893 with a violent seizure of power from Queen Liliʻuokalani, which was backed by the United States Marines. Before this, most of the crown lands were maintained in a relatively unchanging and productive manner by their commissioners. There were a number of factors and preceding events that led to the end of the Kingdom of Hawaiʻi, much of which is intimately connected with the United States of America.

One of the more impactful pieces of legislation that was passed was the 1874 Nonjudicial Mortgage Act, which effectively allowed a lender to auction off the borrower's land deed in the event that the mortgagee had fallen behind in payments. This auction could be carried out without any judicial oversight and resulted in many *Kuleanas* (land titles and rights from the Kuleana Act of 1850) passing from native hands to foreign ones. Moreover, the phenomenon of "adverse possession" also meant that many natives lost their lands to sugar plantation corporations. Adverse possession meant that if a party utilized a part of the land against the interests of the land's legal owner for an extended period of time, the land could be obtained from its original owner. The problem was that the time period for adverse possession to take effect was unusually short in regards to Native Hawaiian land, being only five years long. During this time, King Kalakaua worked closely with the Americans to promote the development of sugar plantations to secure Hawai'i's future. The collapse of some whaling fleets in the north and less traffic to the Hawaiian Islands were also impetuses for Hawai'i to find and develop its own resources. All in all, the number of sugar plantations in Hawai'i increased from twenty to over sixty in just five years. After David Kalakaua turned against American interests and began focusing on Hawaiian nationalism, a secret organization called the Hawaiian League began working to institute a new government in the Hawaiian Islands by any means necessary. The members of this organization were almost all Caucasians, and they also played major roles in the overthrow of the kingdom in 1893. Upon uniting with the Honolulu Rifles, an all-Caucasian civil militia, they outmaneuvered King Kalakaua and gained control of the city. King Kalakaua called on the ministers of Britain, France, Japan, and Portugal for help and even offered to hand over the Kingdom of Hawai'i in exchange for protection and control, but they refused to intervene.

The Hui Aloha ʻAina o Na Kane, or the Hawaiian Patriotic League for Men, who would petition against the eventual annexation, circa 1893.
https://commons.wikimedia.org/wiki/File:Hui_Aloha_%CA%BB%C4%80ina_o_Na_Kane.jpg

Severely outgunned and under threat of assassination, King Kalakaua was forced to accept a new Cabinet and complete the new Constitution of 1887, which would eponymously become known as the Bayonet Constitution, as it was signed under duress. Shortly after this, Pearl Harbor began to be militarized and developed as a naval base for the United States. After the Bayonet Constitution was imposed upon him, King Kalakaua continued his duties, even though the limitations of the new constitution frustrated his people and brought about staunch and vocal opposition. Men had to meet certain conditions before they could vote, and the actions of the king had to be approved by the Cabinet, which included a number of foreigners. Debates were had about whether the handing over of Pearl Harbor to the United States would help prevent annexation or further embolden foreign powers.

David Kalakaua passed away in 1891 while he was traveling to Washington to meet with Hawaiian ambassador Henry Carter to discuss the 1890 McKinley Tariff, which would nullify most of the free trade agreements of the previously signed Reciprocity Treaty. He was succeeded by his sister, Liliʻuokalani, who had already served as queen regent during one of

King Kalakaua's earlier trips. She continued her brother's fight to preserve the independent Kingdom of Hawai'i but was ultimately overthrown. She, too, fought to dismiss the reforms and revisions that were driven by the 1887 Bayonet Constitution, writing that the 1887 Constitution had been imposed by "aliens determined to coerce my brother."

Upon her becoming the queen, Queen Lili'uokalani received well over six thousand petitions and letters from all over Hawai'i, urging her to create a new constitution. This was an impressive number since it was more than two-thirds of the 9,500 or so registered voters of the land. Scholars and community leaders have estimated it to be very close to the entire population of native-born and half-native people. Such a new constitution would have allowed Hawai'i great power over its own authority and autonomy, allowing the monarch to appoint and remove members of the Cabinet and limit voter rights to naturalized and Native Hawaiians, removing much of the voting block of temporary residents.

A digitally colored and restored work of a photograph of Queen Liliʻuokalani, circa 1887. *Digital work by Mark James Miller from a photograph taken by Walery, London, Eng. (1887), CC BY-SA 3.0 <https://creativecommons.org/licenses/by-sa/3.0>, via Wikimedia Commons https://commons.wikimedia.org/wiki/File:Liliuokalani_Restored_2.jpg*

Some members of the queen's Cabinet had refused to sign her newly proposed constitution, and this was an opportunity for a small group called the Annexation Club to begin movements toward the annexation of Hawaiʻi by the United States of America. The overthrow was essentially led by a number of American businessmen who had become immensely wealthy from Hawaiʻi's sugar plantations. After a long period of planning and laying the political and legislative framework before hostilities ensued, these men won the support of the United States of America. On January 16th, 1893, the main coordinating American political representative, John Leavitt Stevens, effectively secured the island of Oahu with approximately 162 armed soldiers. They placed Queen Liliʻuokalani under house arrest. The military presence of the warship USS *Boston* also helped secure American buildings like the US Consulate and Arion Hall.

It was only in 1993, one hundred years after the overthrow, that the United States Congress acknowledged and admitted to the fact that US military and diplomatic officials had played an essential role in facilitating the overthrow of the Kingdom of Hawai'i. The power vacuum that was left was temporarily filled by the Provisional Government of Hawaii, which consisted of the coup leaders. After approximately a year and a half, the Provisional Government of Hawaii gave way to the Republic of Hawaii, which was a sovereign state that was not officially a part of the United States until 1898, even though the Republic of Hawaii had the military and political support of the United States. This meant that the Republic of Hawaii only lasted for about four years. The overthrow was an illegal act that went against international laws and is considered a black mark on the history of the United States of America, even though it issued a formal apology for such activities.

A photograph of US Marines and sailors from the USS Boston occupying Arlington Hotel grounds during the overthrow of Queen Lili'uokalani, 1893.
https://commons.wikimedia.org/wiki/File:USS_Boston_landing_force,_1893_(PP-36-3-002).jpg

Land of Sugar

The incredibly fertile lands and stable, warm climate of Hawai'i proved to be ideal for the growth of sugarcane, which would eventually lead to the dominance of sugarcane over Hawaiian agriculture and sugar exports' iron-clad hold on the Hawaiian economy and overseas interests. Beginning in the 1820s onward, sugar plantations cropped up on the islands of O'ahu, Maui, Kaua'i, Moloka'i, Lana'i, and the Big Island of Hawai'i itself. Over the next one hundred years, sugar production from Hawai'i would grow from under fifty thousand tons of sugarcane to well over half a million tons.

This had several effects. The first was a huge influx of immigrant labor to help cope with the demands of a rising sector, especially since growing, harvesting, and processing sugarcane was a labor-intensive process. Tens of thousands of laborers were contracted from Japan, China, the Philippines, Puerto Rico, and Korea. Hawai'i's population swelled by over 300,000 people over this time and resulted in the percentage of Native Hawaiians dropping to about 10 percent of the total population by the 1900s. It was said that a good tradesman could depend on being gifted some land, along with a native wife, if he was productive and stayed. Sanford Dole, whose relatives would eventually found the Dole Food Company we know today, also wrote and supported the need to increase Hawai'i's population, whether by increasing the flow and residency of immigrant labor or by encouraging current residents to have large families. His view was that the islands would never reach their full productive power without occupying them to a much greater extent.

A photograph of Chinese contract laborers working on a sugar plantation, circa the late 1900s.
https://commons.wikimedia.org/wiki/File:Chinese_contract_laborers_on_a_sugar_plantation_in_19th_century_Hawaii.jpg

During the early 1920s, the Hawaiian Sugar Planters' Association's recruiters would examine the hands of Filipinos who wanted to work with them; only those with the distinct hardened and callused palms of farm and field workers would be accepted. Filipino workers would come to work on Hawai'i's sugarcane fields, dairy industries, and sugar mills. Some of them would work for over thirty years, eventually retiring and settling in Hawai'i as permanent residents. Workers would often be seen as lesser by Caucasian business-owners, especially if they were of obviously different ethnic backgrounds. Some plantation owners and foremen would call workers out by their identification numbers, even though some of them would protest and ask to be called by their names.

A bronze sculpture of various plantation workers at the Old Sugar Mill Monument, Kauaʻi, Hawaiʻi, a work done by Jan Gordon Fisher.
https://commons.wikimedia.org/wiki/File:Koloa-old-sugar-mill-monument-sculpture.JPG

Significant environmental degradation and pollution also resulted from the proliferation of sugarcane plantations. The islands suffered not only from the pollution of coal-burning and iron smelting but also from deforestation due to a ravenous need for both timber and wood fuel. All of this was further exacerbated by a relative lack of fresh water on the islands, as ocean-derived water sources contain salt. Owing to the fact that sugarcane is a crop that requires an immense amount of water to grow and farm, the plantation boom led to forests being cleared and tunnels being constructed to aid in freshwater procurement. Water catchment areas in the mountains were diverted toward the plantations, and deep wells were dug. Even with improvements in technology and efficiency, it took over one ton of water to produce one pound of refined sugar.

Many American businessmen would seize the chance to buy and invest in Hawaiian lands for the purposes of setting up sugar or pineapple plantations. Californian sugar magnate Claus Spreckels came to Hawaiʻi in 1876 and negotiated a very controversial and tenuous deal with Princess Ruth Keʻelikolani, a descendant of the

Kamehameha line. This allowed him to acquire thousands of acres of land. Another famous and notable American that would contribute heavily toward the Westernization of the Hawaiian Islands was Sanford Dole, who would serve as the only president of the Republic of Hawaii. Sanford was raised in Protestant missionary schools, and his father was the principal at what would eventually come to be known as the Punahou School. He was appointed as a justice in the Supreme Court of the Kingdom of Hawai'i by King Kalakaua, and his cousin, James Dole, would eventually come to Hawai'i to found the Hawaiian Pineapple Company. This company would later become the Dole Food Company, which is well known even today.

Brochure by the Hawaiian Pineapple Packers' Association, Honolulu, Hawai'i, 1914.
https://commons.wikimedia.org/wiki/File:Hawaiian_canned_pineapple,_1914.png

The United States and Hawai'i actually had an amicable and mutually beneficial relationship leading up to the 1890s. It had established several treaties with the United States that fostered political goodwill and ensured commercial and navigational cooperation between the two nations. Further, President John

Tyler had also issued an official statement in 1842 that included Hawai'i under the Monroe Doctrine, which proclaimed certain acts of European colonialism as a potential act of hostility toward the United States. This meant that the USA recognized the independent existence of Hawai'i and that they would oppose an invasion of the islands by any other power.

In the end, the annexation goal was spurred on by falling sugar prices and the rising belief that the United States must control Hawai'i against other foreign interests and to protect the West Coast of the contiguous United States of America. There was also a perceived air of economic instability and the potential for an economic depression to beset the islands. This spurred Americans like Lorrin Thurston and Minister John L. Stevens to zealously promote and push the idea of annexation abroad, leading to many US politicians to buy into the idea. Stevens asked the US State Department to send additional naval forces to protect American interests and asked Washington to station a warship in Honolulu indefinitely to secure the islands. This was the beginning of a rapid increase in American military might in Hawai'i.

Chapter 7 – World War II and Hawai'i

Hawai'i's role in World War II is complex, deep, and pivotal. Most importantly, the geographic location of the islands of Hawai'i meant that they were both a target of and a boon to whichever superpower of WWII controlled it. Many battles of the Pacific Ocean would later be launched from, headquartered by, and supported through the islands of Hawai'i.

Prior to Hawai'i's contact with the "outside world," its economy was self-sustaining and almost self-contained. After its existence was popularized to the outside world, the Hawaiian Islands' economy underwent a change, as it became the treasured stop at which whalers, fishermen, and voyagers stopped to refuel, restock, and rest. The established history of the usefulness of the islands made it famous around the world and also added to its importance in determining control of the Pacific Ocean. Additionally, the familiarity of the waters, winds, threats, and routes that surrounded the Hawaiian archipelago further increased its international visibility and recognition. Over time, its economy changed to become agricultural, thus supplying the United States of America and other foreign powers with precious produce and goods. This led to

Hawai'i playing more and more into the hands of American political interests, and it eventually became the turning point of the Pacific Ocean conflict.

Suffice to say, Pacific supremacy could not possibly be attained by a large political superpower without some kind of footing in the Polynesian chain, and Hawai'i was at its center. As we've seen from the previous chapter, due to its contact with the United States, the largely isolated archipelago of Hawai'i was transformed slowly but surely into an outpost of the United States, with a focus on the eventual need for military capabilities. Add to the mix the preestablished sugar plantations and vested interests of the markets of the United States of America, and it should come as no surprise that Hawai'i was targeted by the Japanese, eventually leading to the infamous attack on Pearl Harbor.

Caught in between Japan and America

The historical centrality of Hawai'i for Pacific travelers meant that it had long-established relationships with fur traders, whalers, sandalwood traders, and merchants from China, the Americas, and even Europe. Then, mostly due to its availability of fertile land, temperate and suitable climate, influx and abundance of Asian laborers, and the arrival of opportunistic American businessmen, Hawai'i became an immensely productive and popular exporter of sugar, not only for the American market but also for Japan. By the mid-19th century, Hawai'i's location and function in the Pacific simultaneously put it at the crossroads of two global superpowers and made it the most strategic chain of islands to control.

The twenty-year period of tenuous global peace between WWI and WWII saw US-Japan relations slowly worsen, even though the two nations were reasonably amicable to begin with. A series of historical events gradually soured diplomatic relations. In 1924, America placed a quota on Japanese immigration, which included the islands of Hawai'i, and the Great Depression of the 1930s made matters much worse. At the height of tensions, many business leaders, academics, and regional and religious leaders came together to form the Institute of Pacific Relations (IPR), which was conceived as an unofficial attempt to join countries along the Pacific Rim in a cooperative stance and foster the increasingly important idea of a "Pacific Community." A good number of Americans joined, and the idea garnered some support from the surrounding nations, such as the Philippines, Korea, Japan, China, New Zealand, and Canada. Naturally, the organization chose to host its international conference in Honolulu in 1925 to discuss its issues and concerns. Although the IPR eventually dissolved and failed to prevent conflict in the region, it remains a clear and documented case of international interests being aligned to view Hawai'i not merely as a keystone of naval dominance but also of its prospects and potential for economic cooperation.

Eastern Problems for America's West Coast

For a long time, the United States of America focused much of its security concerns on the Atlantic Ocean and the Caribbean. The recognition of the Pacific Ocean as a vitally important front for war was not high on America's list of priorities. Only after Japan's attack on Pearl Harbor did the strategic significance of Hawai'i become a top priority, so much so that the current headquarters for the commander in chief of the US Pacific Command is located in Hawai'i, and it is the central base for US Navy, Air Force, and Army operations for the region.

The buildup of the United States' interest in Hawai'i as a strategic point of military power began with President Theodore Roosevelt and an advisor of his named Alfred Thayer Mahan. Considered one of the most important United States naval figures of the 19th century, one of Alfred Mahan's core influences on American military thought was the emphasis he placed on the significance of the Pacific Ocean for US security. Nowadays, most of his strategic thinking and writings are collectively referred to as "Mahanism," and it typically places great importance on naval power. This would eventually lead to him lending his voice to and arguing in favor of the US annexing Hawai'i, which occurred in 1898. Specifically, the threat of Japan to the US was the key factor in the thinking that placed such military importance on Hawai'i. Along with other popular writers, Mahan wrote about other concerns, such as the Japanese immigrants failing to assimilate with the culture of the United States. These writings both directly and indirectly fueled hysteria around the sensational image of the "Yellow Peril," a racist ideology that targeted people of East Asian descent. This hysteria would eventually bleed over to the islands of Hawai'i, which was home to a large and growing population of Japanese migrant workers.

Photograph of Alfred Thayer Mahan, circa 1897.
https://commons.wikimedia.org/wiki/File:Photo_of_Alfred_Thayer_Mahan.jpg

A mere ten years after the US annexed Hawai'i, construction of a fully-fledged naval base began in Pearl Harbor. During Theodore Roosevelt's presidency, which lasted from 1901 to 1909, he asked for Pearl Harbor to be fortified, and the United States Congress agreed. However, the process was both slow and inadequate, as most US Navy officials and politicians did not share similar worries over the Pacific theater of war. The number of men stationed in Hawai'i saw a sharp increase to over twelve thousand personnel during the First World War but decreased to just below five thousand men afterward.

A 1942 map of the Pacific Ocean, with Los Angeles in the upper right connected to the Hawaiian Islands and Guam, along with Japan situated in the upper left.
https://commons.wikimedia.org/wiki/File:1942_Pacific_Ocean_(30249104613).jpg

The Japanese invasion of Manchuria in 1931 triggered a renewal of forces in Hawai'i. This happened again when the Empire of Japan waged an undeclared war against China in 1937. Signs of impending war with Japan were looming, and all sorts of pressures were building up to an eventual outbreak of conflict. Such pressures would be materially reflected in the lives of Hawaiians as well, including annual blackout drills and exercises for Hawaiian civilians in Honolulu. Civil defense units and outposts began to spring up in rural areas and surrounding military installations. Further, emergency disaster preparations began in 1940, with

Honolulu women being tasked with surgical dressing and wound bandage production. There were also first-aid training sessions held by the local Red Cross. Honolulu saw the establishment of a blood bank, and the city's Schofield Barracks would grow to become one of the largest US Army installations in the world, hosting and fielding over forty thousand troops by 1941. The primary objective of such a large force was to hold and defend Pearl Harbor and, by extension, Hawai'i from Japanese raiders and invaders. Incidents like the bombing of the SS *President Hoover*, the flagship *Augusta*, and the sinking of the USS *Panay* were strong indicators that Hawai'i was going to be sandwiched between two political and military bulldozers.

Pearl Harbor

On December 7th, 1941, Japan launched an attack called the "Hawaii Operation" on the US naval base of Pearl Harbor, Honolulu. Japan intended to cripple the United States' ability to utilize its naval fleet in the Pacific Ocean, as it could potentially interfere with Japan's military maneuvers in Southeast Asia. It is important to note that the attack on Pearl Harbor was but one instance in a coordinated chain of nearly simultaneous attacks planned and executed by the Empire of Japan. Some of these attacks included Japan's invasion of British Malaya (modernday Malaysia), the invasion of Hong Kong from the north, and the invasion of Batan Island, which was Japan's first foray into the Philippines. Unbeknownst to Hawai'i, the US military actually intended to withdraw from the Philippines in the event of an invasion. This withdrawal did indeed happen once the Empire of Japan made its intentions clear with its move on Pearl Harbor, and although Pearl Harbor was the second attack the Japanese made, being half an hour or so behind the invasion of Kota Bharu (the start of the invasion of British Malaya), it was by far the most important and impactful point of attack.

The attack came out of nowhere, and the morning of December 7th can only be described as a scene of utter chaos and confusion. Japan had not declared war on the US, and by all accounts (except for conspiracy theorists), the attack was a complete surprise. Hundreds of Japanese planes bombed and shot the naval base of Pearl Harbor, killing many people and destroying many ships. The ferocity of the battle is well-documented and paints a horrific experience. Oral and eyewitness accounts of Pearl Harbor say that, at first, natives and other residents of Oʻahu thought it was merely some form of routine firing practice, as gunshots were something that people heard often. It wasn't until a superintendent or another person in charge came running while bearing the sobering news that people began to scatter, either to help the defense effort, seek shelter, or warn others. The attack lasted for about an hour and twenty minutes.

A photograph taken just as the USS Shaw, a destroyer ship, exploded from the Japanese attack on Pearl Harbor, December 7th, 1941.
https://commons.wikimedia.org/wiki/File:USS_SHAW_exploding_Pearl_Harbor_Nara_8 0-G-16871_2.jpg

Ultimately, the United States suffered heavy losses in the aftermath of the attack, losing multiple battleships, cruisers, destroyers, and aircraft. US casualties numbered well over two thousand soldiers, sailors, Marines, and civilians. Huge swaths of the docks and many hangars and buildings were either destroyed or damaged. In fact, some of the damage to the buildings is visible even today. Furthermore, hundreds of American aircraft were lost to general-purpose and armor-piercing bombs dropped by Japanese planes, with the overwhelming majority of the aircraft being destroyed while on the ground and in hangars. Due to the chaotic nature of the ambush and the devastation unleashed by the Japanese, American Air Force pilots had immense difficulty in taking off during the attack to fight back. This effectively meant that Japanese planes had full reign over the skies.

A small boat goes to rescue seamen from the burning battleship, the USS West Virginia. Thick smoke chokes the air and water surface.
https://commons.wikimedia.org/wiki/File:USS_West_Virginia2.jpg

The Japanese forces, on the other hand, suffered very few losses. A few smaller submarines were destroyed, and twenty-nine planes were lost, along with sixty-four lives. The entire attack was carried out through two waves of attack planes launched from Japanese aircraft carriers. They had left Hitokappu Bay, which was located to the north of Japan, approximately two weeks prior to the attack. These aircraft carriers were huge ships that were large enough to carry, fuel, and deploy hundreds of fighter and bomber planes. The first Japanese wave was much more successful than the second wave, as the initial attack made the Americans realize they had to prepare and mount an anti-air defense strategy. Japanese torpedoes, bombs, armorpiercing bombs, and high-capacity automatic guns targeted US troops, battleships, aircraft, outposts, and bases to great effect. The attack marked the official entry of the United States of America into the Second World War.

For a long time, Japan's lack of an official declaration of war before launching the attack was portrayed and thought of by many scholars as late. This supposed lateness was thought to be caused by a number of factors, like the United States' inefficiency of diplomatic communications, its complicated bureaucracy, Tokyo's formal message of "peace negotiations were officially at an end" being too long, and other general factors of accidental bumbling and delays. However, the recent uncovering of official documents by Japanese scholar and professor Takeo Iguchi clearly shows that Japan did not comply with international law, as it purposefully and intentionally hid its true intention of war from the United States in hopes of succeeding in their surprise attack. Pearl Harbor was indeed planned and executed as a surprise attack, and its main objective was to cripple and neutralize the Pacific Fleet of the US Navy.

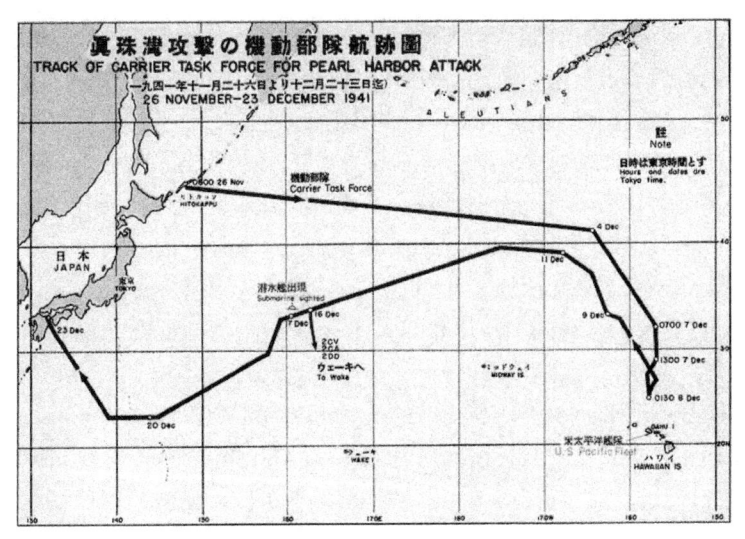

A chart of the route that the Japanese fleet used to approach Pearl Harbor. The arrows indicate their departure from the northern islands (Hitokappu Bay) to Hawai'i (bottom right) and then back to Japan.
https://commons.wikimedia.org/wiki/File:PearlHarborCarrierChart.jpg#file

Aftermath

The most important consequences of the attack on Pearl Harbor were that the United States of America formally entered the Second World War and declared war on Japan. The United States of America was considered to be a neutral player in the Second World War up to that point, as the country was officially bound by the Neutrality Acts that US Congress had passed. The acts were centered around isolationism and non-interventionism, making sure the US did not get involved in the two large conflicts that were going on in Europe and in Asia. On December 11th, 1941, Germany and Italy declared war on the United States of America, and US Congress issued declarations of war against Germany and Italy shortly after that. The attack on Pearl Harbor also united the people of America, with well over 90 percent of the general public supporting the war against Japan.

The Eastern Pacific had not yet seen a threat this global. The previous conflicts between groups of Hawaiians, the War of 1812, the Mexican-American War, the Chinese-Japanese War, the

Japanese-Russian War, and even the First World War had all left impressions on the region but never so directly. Hawai'i was quickly strengthened and fortified by forces and resources sent by the United States. More importantly, the Japanese force had considered their tactical victory of destroying and crippling the American battleships and aircraft to be more complete than it actually was. Accordingly, the Japanese forces did not elect to target Pearl Harbor's navy repair yards, oil reservoirs, fuel storage hangars, submarine docks, dry docks, and headquarter buildings. These facilities proved to be more important to America's Pacific war effort than any ship, allowing the United States to provide logistical support to all of the US Navy's operations through Pearl Harbor.

In Hawai'i, however, the consequences were far quicker to materialize and involved changes to both the structure of daily life and to the demographics of the islands. Concerns about the loyalties of foreign and native-born Japanese people and other suspects were rounded up by military and FBI (Federal Bureau of Investigation) agents. The islands were placed under martial law, and a strict curfew was put into place. Late-night activities were limited due to a military-enforced curfew. These times were scary and stressful for all those living on the islands. Almost all of the islands' inhabitants were subjected to fingerprinting and issued personal papers and identifying documents. Even then, workers and residents with a night pass would sometimes be stopped and subjected to further scrutiny, as soldiers often had difficulty in telling Japanese people apart from Chinese, Filipinos, Koreans, or even Native Hawaiians. Many coastal areas were designated off-limits to the public, and guards were stationed on important shores, beaches, and cliffs.

Early Japanese immigrants that arrived in Hawai'i, 19th century.
https://commons.wikimedia.org/wiki/File:Early_Japanese_immigrants_to_Hawaii.jpg

After the United States of America declared war on the Empire of Japan, it placed over 100,000 Japanese residents in internment camps for fear of misplaced loyalties. This eventually spilled over to Hawai'i, and although the great majority of people of Japanese descent were not shipped off to the internment camps on the mainland, such shipments still happened. Due to the prevalent fear of racial lines being drawn in the war and the threat of the "Yellow Peril," strategies of how to handle Hawai'i's population of Japanese people had to be devised. These plans involved taking certain "strategic hostages" and eventually registered and consigned Japanese people to live in isolated communities. Hawai'i had too many Japanese Americans and Japanese people to merit shipping all of them back to the mainland, and the island was in dire need of labor and expertise. Therefore, Hawai'i was slowly transformed into an internment camp of sorts, with watchful guards, gated communities, and strict laws being enacted. Employment opportunities for women increased dramatically in Hawai'i, as well as in many other parts of the world, as a result of World War II, with job openings for clerks, teachers, nurses, storekeepers, and even mechanics. Men were mostly wanted for physical labor and the war effort, but there was a major emphasis placed on the fact that agricultural work had to continue in spite of war. In fact, there are reliable accounts of plantation workers being refused enlistment because the government knew that the work they were doing in sugar mills and fields was more important to the war effort. Instead, some of the workers were assigned to "home guard" duty and given military ranks, training, and weapons. These men would be attached to the 21st Infantry of the United States Army, but most of them would never be shipped out. Workers would also "bleed" into the surrounding jobs, such as working in the plantation's hospital, assisting in the morgue, helping out with office and administrative duties, and working in foodservice. Hawai'i itself would not see any more attacks or battles for the remainder of World War II, and it was governed through the war with a military government, which was led by three military governors: Walter Short, Delos Emmons, and Robert Richardson Jr.

A call for nurses and nurse's aides from the Office of Emergency Management, dated between 1941 and 1945.
https://commons.wikimedia.org/wiki/File:Air_raid_in_Hawaii_-_Red_Cross_-_NARA_-_513770.jpg

Chapter 8 – Modern Hawai'i

Hawai'i was considered a territory of the United States throughout the Second World War, and most, if not all, aspects of its governance were determined by a military government. Food and fuel were rationed, with priority given to the defenders, watch guards, soldiers, and sailors. Television, radio, and newspapers were censored, edited, and controlled by the Americans to stop enemy propaganda from spreading to the Hawaiian people. Trade, markets, and businesses were sometimes nationalized and, at other times, controlled and regulated to aid the war effort. Even courts, juries, and witnesses were beholden to the military effort, resulting in different American federal departments clashing over conflicting interests over the lands of Hawai'i as the Second World War raged on.

Political Transition

Before World War II, in 1900 to be specific, the United States Congress enacted the Hawaiian Organic Act, which was a piece of legislation that established the Territory of Hawaii and provided it with a constitution and governmental footing. As linguistic orthography was nowhere near as advanced back then as it is today, the more important American political documents have Hawai'i spelled as "Hawaii" without diacritics. Thus, the slight pause in the traditional Hawaiian pronunciation of the name is missing. (As you have noticed throughout the book, we have opted to use the traditional spelling unless Hawaiʻi is being used in a proper name, such as the State of Hawaii or the Republic of Hawaii.) The act would eventually be replaced by the Hawaii Admission Act in 1959, through which Hawaiʻi would gain statehood and join the United States of America as a state.

The martial law that had governed the islands of Hawaiʻi during the Second World War left a thirst for basic liberties in its wake. Toward the end of the war in 1944, as the Allied forces bolstered their hold on the Pacific theater, a transition out of martial law slowly took place. In an approximately two-year-long transitional phase, where extremely restrictive laws were progressively loosened, a movement toward a more democratic state of affairs began. Part of the driving force of this democratic movement was the realization and emphasis on the fact that Hawaiʻi had never voluntarily ceded political power to the United States of America and was, in effect, taken over by force.

The Republican Party of the United States had held power over the islands of Hawaiʻi since the Bayonet Constitution, and many sugar plantation oligarchs also retained vast amounts of land and political influence. In the face of rising racial tensions and awareness of discriminatory practices and policies, one particular politician would rise to the forefront and become the most influential politician in the affairs of Hawaiʻi for nearly two decades. That politician was John Anthony Burns, and his political legacy is undoubtedly significant. Among the American officials who came to govern Hawaiʻi, he is seen as a benevolent politician who, for the most part, had the interests of Hawaiʻi at heart and brought about many improvements and valuable changes to Hawaiʻi and her people.

John A. Burns, second governor of Hawaii, in his meeting with President Lyndon B. Johnson, February 6th, 1966.
https://commons.wikimedia.org/wiki/File:John_A._Burns_1966.jpg

John Burns was born in Montana and moved to Hawai'i in his early twenties, finding work as a police officer. When the war with Japan broke out, he was promoted to the head of the Honolulu Police Department's Espionage Bureau and tasked with vetting the Japanese population of Hawai'i. Through this assignment, John Burns would come to know the Japanese and Native Hawaiian communities very well, which proved helpful in shaping his later policies. By the end of World War II, Burns turned his eyes to a career as a politician, and he had a specific, revolutionary aim in mind. John Burns would build a political coalition that would eventually include many factions of people, including war veterans, labor unions, select members of the Communist Party of Hawai'i, and Japanese Hawaiians and Americans.

Amidst the many people who were racial and social elitists, John Burns was starkly different. He had suffered many tragedies and setbacks in life, and he pushed a new, progressive political front, one in which he sought to put an end to historical privilege as much as possible and give every citizen an equal opportunity to realize their dreams and aspirations. After about eight years, Hawai'i would undergo its Democratic Revolution of 1954, which was led by Burns himself, and he would go on to win Hawai'i's election for governor. Burns would go on to be reelected two more times in 1966 and 1970. John Burns was also elected as Hawai'i's delegate to Congress and is credited with many things, including spearheading the movement for Hawai'i's statehood, reinvigorating multiple economic sectors, and drastically improving and expanding Hawai'i's educational institutions. John Burns sadly passed away in 1973 after battling cancer. His death saw an outpouring of praise and adulation that had not been seen since the days of King Kalakaua himself.

The movement to break from the Territory of Hawaii came forward as a series of elections that pressured the existing Hawaii Republican Party. There were mass protests, general strikes, and acts of civil disobedience. Labor union strikes and the people's demands played a major role in defining the economic pressures that would allow the Hawaiian people to have more influence over their own political fate. Over time, these events would eat away and greatly diminish the power of sugarcane plantation corporations and the Big Five Oligopoly. The Big Five were five agricultural companies that mainly focused on sugarcane and fruit plantations, although nowadays, they have mostly diversified their companies.

Early organizations of this push against the oligarchs and established business hierarchy were kept as an underground movement in order to prevent it from being quickly crushed. As it gathered momentum, strikes were arranged and carried out, often along ethnic lines. Due to the disunity amongst ethnic groups, companies could sometimes hire a different ethnic camp to help fill labor gaps when their original laborers went on strike. Many different factions and political groups rose and fell, including the fall of more communist and far-left parties. The Democrats began to win many more territories than the Republicans, and the push for statehood began shortly after. Outside of John Burns's contribution, politically astute and educated Hawaiians came together under the banner of the Democratic Party and began fighting within the construct of the American two-party system. They had reasoned that true political power and sovereignty over their native lands were closed to them as long as Hawai'i was a territory, and they fueled the push toward statehood.

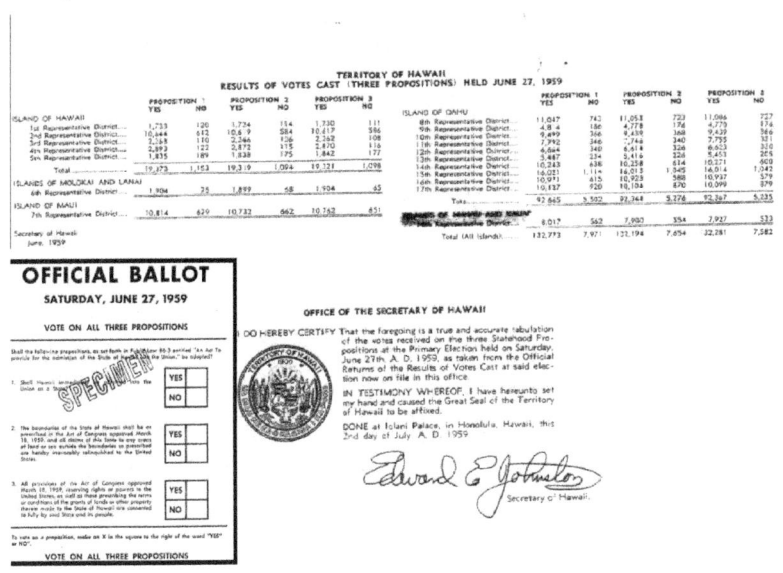

A composite image consisting of the results of the referendum (top), the official statehood vote ballot (bottom left), and the certification from Secretary of Hawaii Edward E. Johnston (bottom center).

https://commons.wikimedia.org/wiki/File:Hawaiivotesinset.JPG#file

The push for statehood was not something new, even though it took a long time to finally achieve it. In the Treaty of Annexation of 1854, there is a clause expressing the early drafters' intentions to seek statehood at the earliest possible time. The political powers of Washington, DC, had shown little to no interest in giving Hawai'i statehood, and the opposition to Hawai'i's statehood used fears of communism as a mask to further their agenda. By 1956, good political maneuvering and coalition building had all but eliminated any communist concerns and brought many other issues to the forefront, making it strikingly harder to ignore the rising movement. Hawai'i's messenger, John Burns, arrived at Washington to find both the House and the Senate working with the Democratic majorities. Famously, John Burns brought and delivered the best of Hawaiian products like flowers, sugar products, and pineapples to congressional offices to help further his cause. After more vigorous lobbying, Congress passed the Admission Act, and a referendum was given to the Hawaiian people on whether to remain a US territory or to accept the new Hawaii Admission Act. The vote showed that 94 percent favored statehood. The Admission Act would be signed into law by President Dwight D. Eisenhower in 1959, admitting Hawai'i into the Union and making Hawai'i the most recent state to join the United States as of this writing.

The Second Hawaiian Renaissance

The First Hawaiian Renaissance is generally categorized as the initial push toward nationalism and revival of traditional Native Hawaiian customs, language, and practices. Scholars often quote this push as having started with King Kamehameha himself, but they also always specifically mention King Kalakaua, as he took significant steps to push Native Hawaiian culture into the modern age. An important instance of his steps to do so was when he replaced the Christian national anthem with "Hawai'i Pono'i," which remains its state song today. In particular, he commissioned the recording of hundreds of Hawaiian chants and recitations of myths and legends, such as the Kumulipo creation myth.

An official embraces the statue of King Kamehameha I during the lei-draping ceremony on King Kamehameha Day.
Anthony Quintano from Honolulu, HI, United States, CC BY 2.0 <https://creativecommons.org/licenses/by/2.0>, via Wikimedia Commons https://commons.wikimedia.org/wiki/File:King_Kamehameha_Day_Lei_Draping_Ceremony_Hawaii_(35194486386).jpg

The Second Hawaiian Renaissance was much more recent and was definitely driven from a musical perspective, which explains much of Israel Kamakawikoʻole's deep, influential legacy (his work will be discussed in the following chapter). The movement started in the late 1960s and saw a resurgence in Native Hawaiian music and Native Hawaiian artistry, along with a reinvigoration of local and academic interests in Hawaiian linguistics and language. Pidgin, also known as Creole, began to be studied and analyzed in earnest, as it bore incredibly important clues about linguistic universals and language creation. Additionally, other investigations and studies about traditional Native Hawaiian crafts and skills started gaining ground.

Naturally, Hawaiian literature and native-written poetry began gaining ground too, and they subsequently reinforced the Second Hawaiian Renaissance, as the literature often mentioned and explored the people of Hawaiʻi's past cultures and lost arts.

Fortunately, this movement also rediscovered and preserved the previous works of writers like David Malo, John Papa ʻIʻi, Kepelino, and Samuel Kamakau. This helped cement an understanding of old Native Hawaiian life and also spurred a generation of reconstructivist art like Hawaiian *kapa* (barkcloth tapestries), Hawaiian tattoos, feather capes, religious petroglyphs, and even hula itself. In fact,

Hawaiʻi became the first state in the United States of America to pass a law for "Percent for Art," in which large-scale projects and development plans needed to include a small percentage of space and funds for public art.

Forestry and land restoration efforts were also renewed, and places that were previously polluted or over-farmed began to be stewarded properly. This began in earnest on a federal level after the National Environmental Policy Act was passed in 1969, which was soon followed by similar laws being passed in different states. Then, work began on determining locations of critical habitats for endangered and threatened species and implementing recovery plans and advisory teams, much of which is continued to this day. Sadly, many Hawaiian forest birds, tree snails, and different plant life are already extinct, but encouragingly and unexpectedly, various different branches of the US military have incorporated environmental protection specialists into their personnel, and land preserves have been set aside on military bases for protecting and monitoring certain species.

Hawaiian arts, including the Hawaiian dance forms of hula, were brought back by Kalakaua's reforms and saw another resurgence with the Second Hawaiian Renaissance. Hollywood prominently featured hula, even though it was a commercialized and watered-down version of the dance, and it spread quickly through the Western world. Tourism spiked with the renewal of Native Hawaiian art forms. Hawaiian and resident artists like Herb Kawainui Kane, Keichi Kimura, Brook Kapukuniahi Parker, Hon

Chew Hee, and Ogura Yonesuke Itoh brought forth many beautiful and soulful Hawaiian depictions of sailing, ocean culture, native peoples, volcano landscapes, and many other facets of Hawaiʻi.

The Hawaiian Sovereignty Movement

More modern times have seen a resurgence in the movement for Hawaiʻi to regain more of its lost sovereignty, a grassroots movement that has been named the Hawaiian sovereignty movement. This push comes through many different lenses: economic, intellectual, political, historical, and social. In essence, the movement seeks some form of reparations or reformation from the United States of America due to the fact that Hawaiʻi was taken from its native rulers via illegal and forceful means. The issues that stem from Hawaiʻi being governed by the US have also added to the movement, citing problems like homelessness, lack of social mobility, real estate inflation, gentrification, poverty, and other issues that affect the islands of Hawaiʻi.

As Hawaiians regained their political and economic standing, the populace began to educate itself and organized to push back against the rulings of Washington, DC, due to the fact that federal regulations often did not sufficiently account for Hawaiian people and Hawaiʻi-specific problems. For example, even though the sugarcane and pineapple oligarchy had been largely neutered when compared to their golden days of power, many American magnates and businessmen still held sway over massive plots of land. These groups still had considerable monetary and political power and inevitably contributed to driving the urbanization and commercialization rates up past what Native Hawaiians could cope with. As the Hawaiian people regained their voice, it became more and more obvious to all onlookers that they should have more control over their own natural resources.

The Hawaiian flag, originally used in the days of the Kingdom of Hawai'i but turned upside down to symbolize Hawai'i's distress. This version of the flag is used by the Hawaiian sovereignty movement.
https://commons.wikimedia.org/wiki/File:Flag_of_Hawaii_Hawaiian_sovereignty.svg

Part of the Hawaiian sovereignty movement that remains highly relevant today is the comparison between the rights of Native Americans and the rights of Native Hawaiians. Native Americans, along with Native Alaskans, possess constitutionally-enshrined rights to selfdetermination that Native Hawaiians largely do not. Although the US has, in modern times, recognized the rights and sovereignty of Native Hawaiians to mostly govern themselves and their islands, this recognition has not been made explicit. This lack of a clear-cut understanding and written legislation is a point of contention that continues even today, with many Hawaiian sovereignty groups fighting the US with awareness, protests, and the law.

Tourism and Commercialization

Tourism has become an important part of Hawai'i's economy, especially from the start of the 20th century onward. More recently, the market and awareness behind Hawai'i's tourism have matured, with more emphasis on responsible ecological tourism, proper native and historical representations, and genuine cultural experiences. With the United States Army having a large and significant presence on Hawai'i, transportation options were never an issue to people once tourism began taking off, with its roots being laid pre-World War II. Hawaiʻi was promoted as an exotic getaway that was still strongly American. The aesthetics of Hawaiʻi focused on flowers, sunlight, beaches, surfing, exotic dancers, and general tropical-paradise-themed elements. Although advertising the islands of Hawaiʻi as such undoubtedly drew many curious visitors, it painted a false narrative that would perpetuate itself through the decades to come.

Famous Hawaiian activist and author Haunani-Kay Trask wrote that even though many Americans had heard of Hawaiʻi, with some even having visited it, few knew of how Hawaiʻi came to be territorially incorporated and economically and politically subordinate to the United States. She goes on to remark that the vast system of capitalist tourism shows Hawaiʻi to millions of tourists every year but fails to show the true face of Hawaiʻi to any real percentage of those tourists. This pushback against the attitude of profit-centric tourism has slowly begun to gain recognition, making Hawaiʻi not just a fantasy getaway land that happens to be five hours from California by plane but an island nation with a rich history and diverse people.

Proponents and educators stress that such awareness is crucial for helping fight factually incorrect yet established stereotypes and misconceptions about Hawaiʻi and also prevent the further erosion and destruction of Native Hawaiian culture, historical artifacts, and land. For the past few decades, many business corporations and tourist industries have consistently pushed the case for more hotels, golf courses, and tourist-friendly showcases of cherry-picked facets of local culture. These campaigns often come at the cost of ecologically or historically important land, and they unavoidably increase real estate prices at artificial rates, resulting in gentrification. Nowadays, historians, activists, and scholars are utilizing modern technological platforms to reach out and show that Hawaiʻi is much more than that. Ecological studies, educational institutions, and local organizations have played and will continue to play key roles in combating the watering down of Hawai'i as merely a vacation-destination island.

Chapter 9 – Notable People of Hawai'i

Akebono Taro

Chadwick Haheo Rowan is a Hawaiian athlete that began playing basketball as a center due to his immense height of six feet eight inches (203 centimeters) and his strength. He later went on to become Akebono Taro, the first non-Japanese-born sumo wrestler to attain *yokozuna* status, the highest rank in sumo.

For a brief period, he attended Hawaii Pacific University but flew to Japan when he was nineteen years old to start training in sumo at the Azumazeki stable ("stable" refers to a training house for sumo wrestlers). Chad Rowan then took on the *shikona* (sumo ring name) of Akebono, which means "new dawn" in Japanese.

His massive height, size, and strength soon made it obvious that he was a force to be reckoned with, rising rapidly through the sumo ranks. Upon reaching the top competitive division of sumo, he was awarded a special prize for defeating a *yokozuna*, a feat few beginner wrestlers ever manage to pull off. His impressive stature and size made him an instantly recognizable wrestler and helped boost the popularity of sumo overseas and within Japan. He, along with another incredibly famous Hawaiian sumo wrestler named Konishiki Yasokichi, were the pioneers in pushing foreign-born sumo wrestlers into the limelight. Konishiki would be the first non-Japanese sumo wrestler to reach the *ozeki* rank, but he would be denied a promotion to *yokozuna*.

Akebono's strong performances and championship wins in the 1990s eventually won him a *yokozuna* promotion. The rank of *yokozuna* is the highest possible rank of sumo champions, and it comes with special privileges and recognition. His reign as a *yokozuna* lasted eight long years and saw him win the championship eight more times, marking him as a strong contender and fan favorite. He became a Japanese citizen during this time.

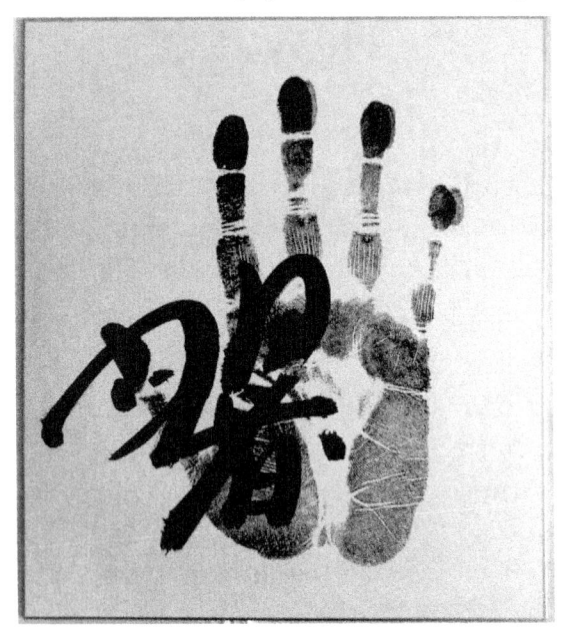

Official Tegata (handprint and signature) of Akebono Taro.
Jeangigot, CC BY-SA 4.0 <https://creativecommons.org/licenses/by-sa/4.0>, via Wikimedia Commons https://commons.wikimedia.org/wiki/File:Akebono_original_tegata.jpg

Akebono's promotion was a groundbreaking moment in Japanese sumo, as it was once considered an unspoken rule that only Japanese-born wrestlers would be eligible for *yokozuna* status. The Yokozuna Deliberation Council had seen Akebono conduct himself with the dignity and humility necessary for such an exalted rank, even though they had previously turned down Konishiki for *yokozuna* promotion. Akebono's genuine passion for both the sport and the Japanese culture was obvious to many spectators, and he was even given the honor of representing Japan in the opening ceremony of the 1998 Winter Olympics after his fellow *yokozuna*, Takanohana Koji, fell ill.

Akebono's and Konishiki's contributions to the proliferation of Japanese sumo overseas and the gradual change in attitudes and perceptions toward non-Japanese wrestlers helped pave the way for many other *yokozuna* who were to come after them.

Barack Obama

Barack Obama was elected the forty-fourth president of the United States and served two terms from 2008 to 2016. He ran as a candidate for the Democratic Party and secured a win against his main opponents from the Republican Party, John McCain and Mitt Romney, respectively.

Both of Barack Obama's parents studied at the University of Hawaii and met each other there in 1960. They eventually got married on the island of Maui and had their only child together, Barack Obama. Obama was born on the island of Oʻahu in the capital city of Honolulu on August 4th, 1961. He spent most of his childhood years in Honolulu and was briefly brought back to Indonesia to visit his stepfather. Obama was schooled at Punahou School, a private school located in Honolulu. His life and upbringing were not religious, as his parents and grandparents were largely nonbelievers.

Obama then went on to study law at Columbia University and Harvard Law School. He is an accomplished lawyer, having taught constitutional law at the University of Chicago Law School for over ten years, becoming a senior lecturer. He also practiced law at the law firm of Davis, Miner, Barnhill & Galland, which specialized in civil rights litigation. There, he worked his way up the chain of seniority and ran a class-action lawsuit against Citibank Federal

Savings Bank.

Obama is the first African American president of the United States and served both as a US senator and a state senator from Illinois before that. As the president of the United States, he signed many bills into law that were very impactful, even if the reforms themselves drew criticism. Some examples of these are the Affordable Care Act (also known as Obamacare), the 2009 American Recovery and Reinvestment Act, the Dodd-Frank Wall Street Reform and Consumer Protection Act, and many others.

Official photographic portrait of President Barack Obama.
Pete Souza, CC BY 3.0 <https://creativecommons.org/licenses/by/3.0>, via Wikimedia Commons https://commons.wikimedia.org/wiki/File:Official_portrait_of_Barack_Obama.jpg

Many people cite Obama's presidency as a turning point for race relations in the United States of America. His stance on foreign matters was mixed, ranging from him overseeing the gradual withdrawal of US soldiers in Iraq to presiding over the mission that led to the death of Osama bin Laden. However, Obama also presided and defended PRISM, which was a code name for the program of mass surveillance that was carried out by the National Security Agency. Through this program, internet communications from various US internet companies were collected, stored, and monitored, supposedly for the safety of the American people. Although many portions of his presidential legacy have garnered harsh critiques, Barack Obama is still considered by scholars, political analysts, and historians to be a great president, and he enjoys a high level of popularity even today.

Barack Obama has written that living in Hawai'i allowed him to experience a wide variety of cultures and grow up in a climate of mutual respect. He quotes his mother as a shaping influence on his views, education, and exposure to the civil rights movement of the 1950s and 1960s, especially since the African American population was tiny, even in the ethnically diverse Hawai'i. His presidency has been and still is hailed as a watershed moment in American politics and another step in the correct direction of the American dream being available to all Americans.

Bruno Mars

Bruno Mars was born as Peter Gene Hernandez in Honolulu, Hawai'i, and quickly rose to international fame through his incredible vocal singing skills and wide range of flexible music styles. His work has included the genres of pop, rhythm and blues, funk, soul, rock, and reggae. Early on in life, he was exposed to a wide range of music styles, in particular the work of Elvis Presley. Bruno quotes Elvis and Michael Jackson as key inspirations for his onstage presence and performances. Growing up in Hawai'i and listening to the radio and his father's percussion performances, he was influenced by Hawaiian music and even hula music.

As a child, he was given the nickname Bruno, and later on, he decided to add Mars to make it sound like he was from another planet so that record labels and music companies would stop trying to pigeonhole him into being "the next Enrique Iglesias." His father is of Puerto Rican and Jewish descent, and his mother is Filipino and Spanish, and they met each other while performing in a show. Bruno would go on to become one of the best-selling music artists of all time, with well over 130 million records sold worldwide. He is known for a number of hit singles, including "Grenade," "When I Was Your Man," "Just the Way You Are," and "Uptown Funk." His fame, personality, philanthropy, and musical prowess have earned him multiple prestigious awards, including eleven Grammy Awards, nine American Music Awards, and three Guinness world records.

Bruno Mars, 2021.
LXT production, CC BY-SA 4.0 <https://creativecommons.org/licenses/by-sa/4.0>, via Wikimedia Commons https://commons.wikimedia.org/wiki/File:Bruno_Mars.jpg_by_LXT_production.jpg

After his parents divorced and his father's various businesses eventually failed, Bruno and his family had to move to the poorer neighborhoods of Hawaiʻi. He and his family grew up and worked their way through hard times, but Bruno holds fond memories of Hawaiʻi and regularly visits and holds concerts on the islands. He said that in the years when he was not yet famous, he would receive phone calls from home but remained evasive because he did not want to return to Hawai'i as a failure. He wanted to come back as a success and make his family and community proud of him. He credits much of his stage presence, techniques, and musical evolution to growing up in Hawai'i since he performed and helped out in a lot of shows with his father's band.

Even today, he remains a relevant and sought-after name in the music industry, recording features, remixes, and new albums that continue to break into the Billboard Hot 100. His ambiguous racial features have sometimes made him feel out of place in the music industry but have ultimately only boosted his popularity and appeal. This defiance of categorization has also flowed into his musical style, with retro elements pervading his music tours, diverse dance routines being showcased in his music videos, and unique music-genre fusions becoming typical for Bruno Mars over the years. He has done work centered around providing scholarships to Hawaiians who are venturing into the music industry through partnering with the Hawai'i Community Foundation and the Grammy Foundation. The program helps youths with training, careers, and interactive immersion, and it was established in honor of Bruno's mother.

Bethany Hamilton

Bethany Hamilton is a professional surfer who was born on the island of Kaua'i in 1990. She grew up in Hawai'i and was exposed to the sport of surfing very early on in her life, at the age of three. Most of Bethany's family were surfers too, and they helped nurture Bethany's newfound passion to greater heights. When she was only eight years old, she began to surf competitively, going on to eventually win first place in the 2002 Open Women's Division of the National Scholastic Surfing Association of the United States. Bethany would go on to compete in many other surfing competitions and even win a good number of them.

On October 31ˢᵗ, 2003, while Bethany was going for a morning surf along the beaches and waves of Tunnels Beach, Kauaʻi, she was attacked by a tiger shark that was over twelve feet long. The shark took a huge bite out of Bethany's surfboard and, at the same time, bit off Bethany's left arm. Bethany was lying on her stomach when the attack happened, and she was also talking to her fellow surfer and close friend, Alana Blanchard. The attack left Bethany in shock, and she was rushed to shore by Alana and Alana's brother and father. Bethany lost so much blood on the way to the hospital that she was passing in and out of consciousness. A doctor rushed to save her life and managed to stabilize her. The shark that was responsible for the attack was caught and killed by local fishermen. Undaunted, Bethany returned to surfing despite the extreme trauma of the incident, and she was riding the waves merely one month after the attack.

Bethany Hamilton crushing a wave in 2016.
troy_williams, CC BY 2.0 <https://creativecommons.org/licenses/by/2.0>, via Wikimedia Commons https://commons.wikimedia.org/wiki/File:Bethany_Hamilton_surfing_(sq_cropped).jpg

The attack and Bethany's courage in the face of such a disaster received international coverage from various sources of media. She was invited as a guest onto numerous television shows, including *The Oprah Winfrey Show*, *Good Morning America*, and *The Ellen DeGeneres Show*. Furthermore, she was included in issues of *Time* magazine and *People* magazine with articles that mentioned her unflappable attitude and motivational story. Bethany is a devout Christian and has mentioned that the attack both tested and strengthened her faith in her religion, causing her to reevaluate her life and learn to appreciate every moment of it.

Bethany now has a custom-made board that is much easier to use and control with her right arm, and she continues to surf competitively. She has written several books about her experience, her life, and her faith, slowly developing a career as a motivational speaker and life coach. She has started and runs several outreach and charity programs, notably programs for women and men who have experienced tragic limb loss or amputees. These programs include a focus on cultivating a positive mindset toward life, fitness, and healthy living. Bethany is a mother of three and continues to inspire and educate women and men all over the world.

Duke Kahanamoku

Duke Kahanamoku, whose full name is Duke Paoa Kahinu Mokoe Hulikohola Kahanamoku, was born in 1890 in Honolulu, Oʻahu. His mother was a deeply religious woman, and he was named after his father, who was christened by a visiting bishop. Duke had an impressive stature, being over six feet tall and weighing nearly two hundred pounds. He boasted a physique that matched his athleticism. His build and his ability to conquer huge waves when surfing would earn him the nickname "The Big Kahuna," with *kahuna* meaning an expert. He would go on to work as a law enforcement officer, an actor, a surfboard designer and builder, a janitor, and also a businessman. However, his most famous achievements were in the Olympics, where he would become the first Hawaiian to win an Olympic medal.

Duke Kahanamoku surfing the waves of Waikiki, 1910.
https://commons.wikimedia.org/wiki/File:Duke_Kahanamoku,_Waikiki,_1910.jpg

Duke was an incredible swimmer and surfer, and he went on to win the swimming gold medal for the 100-meter freestyle in the 1912 Summer Olympics that were held in Stockholm, along with a silver medal in the men's 4x200-meter freestyle relay race. He would win gold again in the 1920 Olympics and silver in the 1924 Olympics, effectively placing Hawaiian swimmers on the global map. Moreover, Duke Kahanamoku is widely credited with popularizing surfing and bringing it to Australia and California. His legacy gave the sport the kickstart it needed to become an international phenomenon and pastime, and he is honored with statues in California and Australia. Thanks to his contacts and popularity in California, he starred as a background actor and side character in many Hollywood movies as well. He mostly portrayed Native Hawaiian characters, fostering a new relationship between the shores of Hawai'i and California.

Heroically, in 1925, Duke rescued eight men from a fishing ship that had capsized due to heavy waves and rough seas off the coast of California's Newport Beach. Utilizing his surfboard, Duke swam back and forth from sea to shore, pulling people onto his board and helping them back to shore. This event was one of the many factors that ultimately led to surfboards becoming standard-issue equipment for lifeguards and water-rescue teams. Additionally, he lent his voice in support of Hawai'i's statehood movement and was elected the sheriff of Honolulu, a position he held for twenty-nine years.

Although he was discriminated against for his dark skin and complexion, he was never bitter or resentful. Instead, he carried an aura of confident optimism and calm joy, as noted by many people in their tributes of him after he passed in 1968 at the age of seventy-seven. To all scholars and historians of his life, it is clear that Duke Kahanamoku helped bridge the gap between the United States and Hawai'i. His ashes were scattered into the ocean.

Israel Kamakawiko'ole

Israel Kamakawiko'ole was a Hawaiian musician and singer who achieved international success for his songs and voice. Many music critics comment that Israel's music was quintessentially Hawaiian: simple yet deep and ad hoc in style and flow. Israel credits his uncle, Moe Keale, who was also a Hawaiian musician and ukulele maestro, for having a major influence on his music. An immense man, both literally and spiritually, Israel Kamakawiko'ole stood six feet two inches tall and weighed well over four hundred pounds. His music would grow to become a deeply inspirational, moving, and uniting force for Hawaiians around the world.

Israel, or Iz as he was affectionately and colloquially known, would be exposed to music from a very young age. Around the age of eleven, he would be invited on stage with his ukulele to perform and sing with Hawaiian musician Del Beazley, who noted that the first time he heard Iz perform, the whole room fell silent upon hearing him sing. Together with his older brother, Skippy Kamakawiko'ole, and a few other friends, Israel founded the Makaha Sons, a band that would go on to become very famous and win awards in Hawai'i and overseas.

Unfortunately, Skippy died at the age of twenty-eight of a heart attack, an incident that was likely brought on by his obesity. Israel would go on to leave the band and start his journey as a solo musician, resulting in his first solo album being released in 1990. Afterward, what would become his most famous song, the medley "Somewhere Over the Rainbow/What a Wonderful World," would debut with his album *Facing Future* in 1993. *Facing Future* would go on to become Hawai'i's first-ever certified platinum album, selling over a million copies in the United States alone.

Israel would go on to be awarded Male Vocalist of the Year, Favorite Entertainer of the Year, and Contemporary Album of the Year by the Hawai'i Academy of Recording Arts multiple times over his lifetime. He was known not only for his music; Israel also championed Native Hawaiian rights and independence, both through his lyrics and his words. Iz commented and touched on themes like social status, Native Hawaiian perceptions of themselves, drug abuse, and responsible parenting.

One of his last public appearances would become one of his most memorable and touching performances. In 1996, Israel would attend the Na Hoku Hanohano Award show and perform splendidly, despite being fed oxygen through a thin plastic tube due to his weight now being well over seven hundred pounds. Dressed in black and with sunglasses, Israel gave off an aura of cool composure and followed his song up by talking about his history with music, spreading love, connecting with native ancestry, and condemning drugs. Afterward, he would be pleasantly surprised by an onstage reunion with the Makaha Sons, describing his feelings as "I didn't know what was going on. I just had my eyes closed. I heard Moon's voice [Louis "Moon" Kauakahi] and I opened my eyes and looked to the side and there he was...I was crying, yeah, I was crying. There was a lotta emotions, a lotta feeling of love, an awesome feeling of aloha."

Tragically, the world-famous singer passed away at the young age of thirty-eight in 1997. Israel had struggled with obesity and obesity-related health issues from a very young age, as he absolutely loved starchy Hawaiian foods, although his genetics likely did not help. Diabetesrelated kidney and respiratory problems plagued him throughout the last years of his life, and his health was also further jeopardized by his earlier smoking and drug usage, which started when he was only fifteen. His marijuana usage gave him the "munchies," which further fueled his already large appetite.

Thousands of people attended his funeral at the Hawaii State Capitol to pay their last respects to an artist who was truly larger than life. People waited while standing for hours just to pass by his casket that was fashioned from the Koa tree, a massive tree endemic to Hawai'i. The Hawaiian flag flew at half-staff for the funeral of "The Voice of Hawai'i."

Chapter 10 – Culture of Hawai'i

Hawai'i is famous for many influences that now span the worldwide stage, which is an impressive achievement for the island nation. The products and offshoots of its culture are sometimes so renowned and representative of Hawai'i that it would be a travesty not to include them in this book.

Music and Dance

Ukulele

One of the aforementioned world-renowned Hawaiian objects is an instrument that is indeed world-famous, for it has been used and popularized by musical artists such as the aforementioned Israel Kamakawiko'ole, Taylor Swift, George Harrison of the Beatles, and more. Aside from appearing in countless talent show auditions, this instrument has gained popularity alongside the invention of plastics manufacturing and was exported all over the world. However, the ukulele is more than just a "smaller guitar"; it has been used not only as a symbol of Hawai'i's extensive and rich musical culture and history but also as a political tool, a tourist souvenir, or a sought-after collectible.

Hawaiian hula dancers with a guitar (center) and ukuleles (on either side).
https://commons.wikimedia.org/wiki/File:Hula_dancers,_photograph_by_J._J._Williams_(PPWD-6-4.026).jpg

In the 1920s, anthropologist and ethnomusicologist Helen Roberts was asked by Hawaiian officials to collect, record, and publish traditional and ancient songs, chants, and poems of the Hawaiian Islands. After over a year of work, she had compiled hundreds of records through interviews and trips. One of her most interesting findings was presented in a report that concluded the ukulele not to be of Hawaiian origin, even though it was (and still is) widely associated with Hawai'i by tourists, musicians, scholars, and even the Native Hawaiians. In truth, the ukulele descended from the Madeiran machete, with the word "machete" referring to an instrument, not a broad, heavy knife. It was introduced to Hawai'i by Portuguese immigrants from the island of Madeira, which is located off the coasts of Morocco and Portugal. The

Madeiran machete is an instrument that looks much like the ukulele; in other words, it looks like a small guitar. It is a string instrument that has five metal strings and is traditionally made of wood. This was the template upon which three carpenters would fashion the ukulele and claim to be the inventor of the instrument.

These three immigrant laborers were Manuel Nunes, Jose do Espirito Santo, and Augusto Dias, and they were all registered as cabinet-makers. Being carpenters, they had the necessary skills to begin fashioning a replica or variant of the Madeiran machete. Due to agricultural troubles in Madeira's wine industry around the 1840s, the island's economy took a turn for the worse. By the late 1870s, many people were desperate and destitute. Shortly after that, many of them left to look for better fortunes in a faraway place in the Pacific that was, at the time, called the Sandwich Islands. These islands were a six-month voyage away, but the workers—men and women both—were more than happy to take such a long trip for a chance at a better future. After their labor contracts expired, Nunes, Santo, and Dias went to Honolulu, the thriving city and commercial center of Hawai'i, and sought to make a living there. They all took up work and placed newspaper ads as guitar makers and furniture makers who dealt with stringed instruments and cabinets. Years later, they would each lay claim to being the inventor of the ukulele, but the truth is that they likely co-invented the instrument according to trends of economic demand and rising local popularity and, in the process, influenced each other.

MANUEL NUNES,
Manufacturer of
Guitars, Ukuleles,
TARO PATCH FIDDLES.
Workmanship and Material Guaranteed. Repairing a Specialty.

1130   :————No. 219½ KING St.

An ad placed by Manuel Nunes in a Hawaiian newspaper, September 13th, 1899.
https://commons.wikimedia.org/wiki/File:Ad_-_Manuel_Nunes,_Manufacturer_of_Guitars_and_Ukuleles.jpg

Jose de Espirito Santos

King street. – two doors below Punchbowl

MANUFACTURER OF

Guitars, : Ukuleles,

TARO PATCH FIDDLES.

Workmanship and material guaranteed. Repairing a specialty.

An ad placed by Jose do Espirito Santo in a Hawaiian newspaper, September 13th, 1899.
https://commons.wikimedia.org/wiki/File:Ad_-_Jose_Do_Espirito_Guitars_%26_Ukuleles.jpg

A. DIAS,

Manufacturer of Ukuleles, Taropatch and Guitars.
All kinds of repair work.

1130 Union Street Honoulu.

An ad placed by Augusto Dias in a Hawaiian newspaper, January 10th, 1906.
https://commons.wikimedia.org/wiki/File:Ukulele_Ad_-_Augusto_Dias,_inventor_of_the_ukulele.tif

Nonetheless, the ukulele went on to sell millions of units made in different styles, especially in the USA. One of its charms was that it became a multimedia phenomenon, being played in nightclubs, restaurants, orchestras, and Hawaiian music groups. Mainstream artists of the time like Johnny Marvin, Ernest Kaʻai, and Frank Crumit soon picked the ukulele up and rode the instrument's popularity wave while simultaneously adding to it. The instrument even made it onto Broadway in the musical *Lady, Be Good*. Its spread even had *The New York Times* reporting that Edward, Prince of Wales, had expressed a desire to learn to play the instrument. Further Western coverage of music produced by the ukulele found its unique sound and timbre hard to describe, as it was decidedly different from the machete and the guitar.

In 1922, Manuel Nunes died, and obituaries in Honolulu printed his death and stated that the "inventor of the ukulele" had passed away. These publications were read and reprinted by other newspapers and reporters, eventually leading to wire services transmitting this news to the United States mainland. Newspapers, columnists, and magazines in cities like New York City, Boston, and Los Angeles, just to name a few, would reprint this somewhere in their publications. Whether it was a column here, a paragraph there, or any other fleeting mention, newspapers propagated further references to the ukulele. Additionally, newspaper headlines would emphasize the false fact that a white man had invented the ukulele, not a Native Hawaiian.

A Hawaiian girl with a ukulele, 1912.
https://lt.wikipedia.org/wiki/Vaizdas:Kohala_Seminary_student_with_ukulele.jpg#file

Even as recent as the past two decades, misconceptions, uninformed criticisms, and myths about the ukulele continue to crop up. The "mini-guitar" enjoyed spikes of popularity during the period of the Roaring Twenties (1920-1929), the advent of postwar plastics, and the most recent surge in popularity, which was fueled by artists like Paul McCartney and Bruno Mars, along with thousands of online personalities on YouTube, Instagram, and other video platforms.

Hula

Although many people think of hula as a dance where exotic women wearing leis and grass skirts twirl and dance with their hips, the full scope of hula is much larger and more nuanced than the mainstream stereotype that has come to be associated with the word. Hula is an ancient form of dance, theater, and social and religious expression that traces its history to more than three hundred years ago. Hula has many legends and myths associated with its origins, with one example being that hula was the dance that Hiʻiaka, the sister of the goddess of fire and volcanoes, Pele, used to appease and calm her sister's hot temper. Hula is claimed to have been invented by different islands of Hawaiʻi, and these islands often have differing origin legends about the dance.

A promotional lobby card for an American romantic comedy film, Hula (1927).
https://commons.wikimedia.org/wiki/File:Hula_lobby_card.jpg

Hula can also be a visual dance form that accompanies a chant, called an *oli*, or a song, called a *mele*, where a story is told. Hula is the portrayal, dramatization, and acting out of the events and phenomena of the story. Like other traditional cultural dances around the world, hula is mostly danced by women and boasts a wide range of movements and routines, with most of them featuring a mostly stable upper body and a moving, bending lower body. Even though hula is typically performed by women, there are male hula dancers. In fact, it was considered a great honor to be an accomplished male hula dancer, as it was a sign that an individual would be a great warrior. The early Hawaiians, like other ancient cultures, believed that good dancers made good fighters.

Male Hula dancers in their performance costumes, 2017.
TheRealAnthonySalerno, CC BY-SA 4.0 <https://creativecommons.org/licenses/by-sa/4.0>, via Wikimedia Commons https://commons.wikimedia.org/wiki/File:Hawaiian_Hula_Dancers.png

In recent times, hula has seen a resurgence in academia and popular culture, especially with regards to competition and schooling. Hula-specific schools and groups come from all over Hawai'i to compete and display the most vibrant, rich, technical, and beautiful hula performances. In particular, the Merrie Monarch Festival is a week-long event that features many different facets of Hawaiian culture, including the most prestigious hula competition in the world. The festival honors King Kalakaua, who is credited with starting the First Hawaiian Renaissance and reinvigorating the lost arts and traditions of Hawai'i, especially hula.

Hula dancers practice for many years to compete, and they sport elaborate costumes with bands around their feet and hands that accentuate their movements and poses. Sometimes these bands are made out of decorated gourd rattles that shake and rattle as the dancer moves in rhythm with the beat of the percussion gourd that is traditionally used in hula, called an *ipu*.

Language

Although both English and Hawaiian are listed as Hawai'i's official languages, the vast majority of Hawaiians speak English, with less than 1 percent of Hawaiians being native speakers of Hawaiian. Even though Hawaiian is still an endangered language, it once was at the point of extinction due to the theological, educational, religious, and political pressures of Christian missionaries who arrived on Hawai'i many years ago. Luckily, King Kamehameha III reestablished the importance of the Hawaiian language and used it to encode the 1839 and 1840 Constitutions of the Hawaiian kingdom.

The Hawaiian language is a member of the Austronesian language family, and it is a Polynesian language. Lexical similarities, cognates, and comparative methods are able to linguistically prove the close relationships between Hawaiian and other Polynesian languages like Marquesan, Tahitian, Māori, and many more. These languages are not mutually intelligible but have basic word similarities and short phrases and utterances that can be understood between speakers of each language. Linguistic and genetic sampling that compares the level of comprehension and word similarity between languages supports the migratory and archaeological trends that predict the movements of ancient Polynesian people. Today, Hawaiian is taught in many schools, both public and private, and is maintained by different levels of academic institutions.

Although Hawaiians had no written language prior to Western contact, like many other cultures around the world, Hawaiian morphology and words adapt fairly well to the Latin script, partly because almost all Hawaiian words end in vowels. This writing system was adapted to the Hawaiian language by American

Protestant missionaries, and they added consonants that were absent in the Native Hawaiian language to their alphabet. Although this newly made Hawaiian alphabet was close to one symbol per sound, it still did not allow foreign words to be easily introduced to Native Hawaiians, as the early missionaries were not aware of linguistic phenomena like phonotactics and morphological rules. In practice, many of these foreign words were Hawaiianized, and the remnants of this pattern can be seen in the Hawaiian language even today.

Hawaiian can be learned through a number of modern apps and online books, with language immersion being the most effective method of learning Hawaiian. The language follows the third most common word order of languages, the verb-subject-object word order, like Irish and Scottish Gaelic. Hawaiian also employs different forms of the word "we," distinguishing between the "inclusive we" that includes the person being spoken to and the "exclusive we" that excludes the person being spoken to. Hawaiian managed to escape suppression, especially after the overthrow of the Hawaiian kingdom, and experienced a revitalization along with other aspects of Hawaiian culture during the Hawaiian Renaissances.

Tourism and Popular Culture

Luau

Popularized by the surge of tourism in Hawai'i, a luau refers to a traditional Hawaiian feast and party that includes entertainment, music, and dance. Nowadays, the word has become synonymous with the word *party* and has been used as such in phrases like "a graduation luau,"

"a birthday luau," and "a wedding luau." In ancient times, due to the customs and rituals of *kapu*, men and women were not allowed to feast together and required separate areas for meals.

The luau has its roots as an *'aha'aina*, meaning a "gathering meal," where the serving of meat was the high point of the feast. Contrary to popular belief, meats and entire roasted pigs were not common in Native Hawaiian life, as this was not an abundant resource and was eaten only during special occasions. Nowadays, luau cuisine includes salmon, poke, roasted pigs, poi, beer, fruit cocktail, other roasted meats, and many other delicious dishes.

A tray of food served at a traditional Hawaiian luau featuring corn, yam, bacon, poi, and other side dishes.
The Eloquent Peasant, CC BY-SA 4.0 <https://creativecommons.org/licenses/by-sa/4.0>, via Wikimedia Commons
https://commons.wikimedia.org/wiki/File:Food_at_a_traditional_Hawaiian_luau.png

Luaus were "invented" by King Kamehameha II, who ended the *kapu* surrounding the events and held a feast where he ate alongside women in a symbolic gesture of new societal standards.

The word "luau" itself translates literally to "taro," and the feast takes this name because taro was one of the most common foods that were served at such feasts. Large open fires, clay pits, earthen ovens, and barbecue grills are often seen in luaus, where meat and other foods are prepared. Traditionally, utensils are not used in luaus, and all of the food is meant to be eaten by hand and in a communal setting. These gatherings would be a time for social bonding, collective celebration, bounty sharing, and as a form of religious ritual and thanksgiving. Luaus are often held by the beach or in specific purpose-built spots that are chosen for convenience, accessibility, cleanliness, comfort, and a nearby sunset view.

A photograph of Native Hawaiians at a luau, 1899.
https://commons.wikimedia.org/wiki/File:Hawaii_Luau_from_1899.jpg

The rapid growth of the tourism industry saw luaus become a quintessential part of experiencing Hawai'i, as such events tied together many aspects of the islands. Luaus included Hawaiian music, Hawaiian cuisine, Hawaiian performances, and Hawaiian hospitality. Although some critics have written that the modern-day luau has become over-commercialized and, as a result, is divorced from its native roots and original meaning, the popularity of luaus has remained unaffected. The feasts can vary significantly and, thus, offer very different experiences, with factors including which island the luau is held on, the organizers of the luau, the seasonal availability of foods, and the extent to which the luau follows Native Hawaiian traditions. Nonetheless, luaus remain an extremely popular tourist experience where food, music, friends, and Native

Hawaiian culture mix, and they will continue to thrive for the foreseeable future.

Lei

A lei is a Hawaiian and Polynesian garland that is usually worn around the neck and is a sign of honor, welcome, and friendship. Leis are made and given for a wide variety of reasons, with the most well-known instance being a welcome gift for travelers and tourists when they first arrive in Hawaiʻi. Besides that, leis are made and worn for hula performances, weddings, religious ceremonies, graduations, and school events. Historically, leis have been made and sold to newcomers since before World War II. Locals, along with wives and daughters of interracial marriages, would run stands selling leis, along with tropical fruits and snacks like cooked breadfruit, bananas, plantain fritters, pineapples, and the like. They would work at airports and the waterfront where passenger ships docked or embarked from the port.

Leis could be (and are traditionally still) made from flowers, beads, and seeds. There were stores that stocked lei flowers, beads, strings, tools, and seeds from collectors who sourced the beads and seeds that had washed down from the mountains of Hawaiʻi. Lei makers would drill holes in them and string them on cords and wires. Glass beads, seed hulls, and shells would also be used in certain leis, allowing leis to have an extremely diverse set of styles and looks.

Even paper leis had different types of folded and twisted styles. Some of the leis would incorporate sewing, back-sewing, special twisting techniques, and even knitting. Leis could be all sorts of colors or color combinations. Oral histories of lei makers show that they would take note of which styles and color schemes were most popular with foreigners or army men and make changes accordingly.

Lei sellers would crowd and show off their leis on their arms, trying to entice buyers and tourists because the business was a valuable supplementary source of income for their families. Many would use their backyards to grow different flowers, with some examples being Hawaiian hibiscus, crown flowers, plumerias, carnations, ilima, pikake jasmines, baldheads, and candle flowers. Luxurious and beautiful leis that are thick with real flowers can be immensely time-consuming to create by hand. Many lei makers have to pick certain flowers at specific times of the day, which means they invest lots of time into flower procurement and then even more time into stringing the flowers together. Since lei makers back in the 1800s and 1900s did not have the option of utilizing refrigeration to extend the shelf-life of their product, most leis would only last a few days unless other preservative measures were taken. Leis continue to be a central and prominent element of Hawaiian and Polynesian culture and aesthetics.

Hula girls wearing leis, some younger and some older, at Kapiolani Park, presumably all from the same halau (school for learning hula).
Hakilon, CC BY-SA 3.0 <https://creativecommons.org/licenses/by-sa/3.0>, via Wikimedia Commons https://commons.wikimedia.org/wiki/File:Hula-M%C3%A4dchen.jpg

Conclusion

Summarily, there is much more to Hawai'i than meets the eye, from their awesome ancient navigating and sailing prowess to their lost great *heiaus* of yore. Hawai'i has always been and will very likely continue to be a unique and important point of interest for the entire Pacific Rim and the ocean itself. We are only now beginning to see the beauty and diversity that such an island nation offers in terms of island hopping, coral reefs, migration patterns, and multiclimate environments. Hawai'i is an ecological treasure that is rare, isolated, and more vulnerable than people are aware of. This book is just one small step in raising awareness of the precarious nature that, sadly, many island nations face in terms of their future ecological stability.

Hawai'i has taken this geographical and natural richness and supplied it with a narrative that is equally as rich and detailed. Their ancient mythologies and ideologies are quite unlike any other in the world, arising in a history almost devoid of wider civilizational influences. Its people have faced enormous historical challenges, from oppression and annexation all the way to germ-driven genocide. Fortunately, its people have survived and are uncovering their deep roots, an effort that is gaining traction. From its royal lineages and families of gods, Hawai'i's people have much to look forward to. They have even more to share with the world, as its famous peoples and artifacts have already proven to inspire and create change throughout the world. Undoubtedly, its future is fertile and almost unfailingly positive if Hawai'i's politics, government, and socioeconomics serve its people.

Although this book touched upon most of Hawai'i's finest moments and times of trouble, we hope that our reader takes with them a sense of wonder, hunger, and joy and learn more about one of the world's most hidden gems nestled in the middle of the Pacific Ocean. If you ever visit the archipelago of Hawai'i, we hope that this book will provide you with an awareness and an understanding of the stories that run through the lands and imbue it with *mana*, the spiritual energy and life force that runs through its people. Hawaii was, is, and will very likely continue to be a beautiful place of deep import, and we hope to have shared a bit of that beauty with you through our writing.

Here's another book by Captivating History that you might like

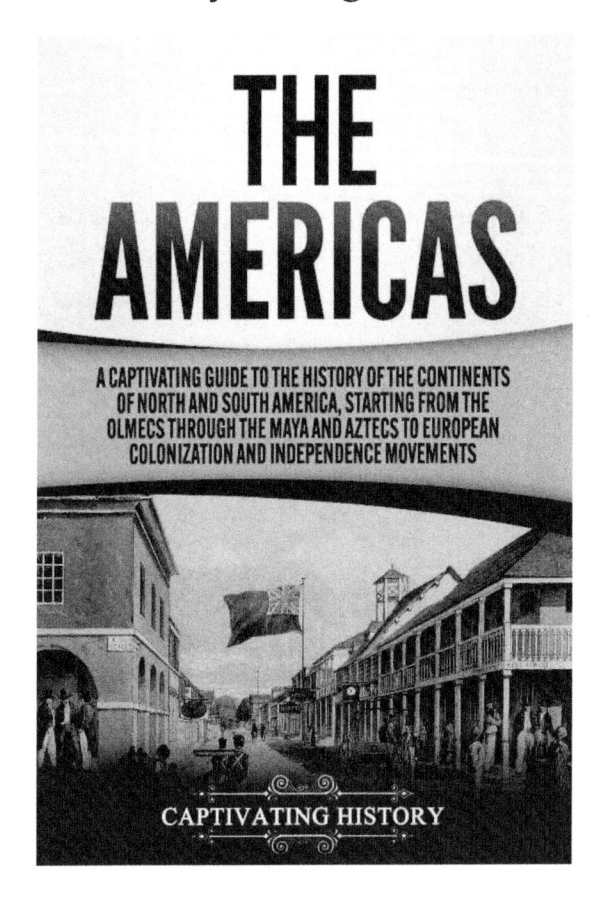

Free Bonus from Captivating History (Available for a Limited time)

Hi History Lovers!

Now you have a chance to join our exclusive history list so you can get your first history ebook for free as well as discounts and a potential to get more history books for free! Simply visit the link below to join.

Captivatinghistory.com/ebook

Also, make sure to follow us on Facebook, Twitter and Youtube by searching for Captivating History.

References

Michi Kodama-Nishimoto. *Talking Hawai'i's Story: Oral Histories of an Island People.* 2009.

Jim Tranquada & John King. *The 'Ukulele: A History.* 2012.

Edward D. Beechert. *Working in Hawai'i: A Labor History.* 1985.

William D. Westervelt. *Legends of Gods and Ghosts.* 1915.

Martha Beckwith. *Hawaiian Mythology.* 1940.

William DeWitt Alexanders. *A Brief History of the Hawaiian People.* 1891.

Robert P. Dye & Bob Dye. *Hawai'i Chronicles: World War Two in Hawai'i.* University of Hawai'i Press. 2000.

Jon Thares. *Hawai'i at the Crossroads of the U.S. and Japan before the Pacific War.* 2008.

Alan C. Ziegler. *Hawaiian Natural History, Ecology and Evolution.* 2002.

Noenoe K. Silva. *Reconstructing Native Hawaiian Intellectual History.* 2017.

Dan Cisco. *Hawaiʻi Sports, History, Facts and Statistics.* 1999. Haunani-Kay Trask. *From a Native Daughter.* 1993.

Jon Van Dyke. *Who Owns the Crown Lands of Hawaiʻi?* 2007.

Christopher Grandy. *Hawaiʻi Becalmed, Economic Lessons of the 1990s.* 2002.

Daniel Marston. *The Pacific War Companion: From Pearl Harbor to Hiroshima.* 2003.

Tom Dye. "Population Trends in Hawaiʻi before 1778." The Hawaiian Journal of History. 1994.

Carol A. MacLennan. *Hawaiʻi Turns to Sugar: The Rise of Plantation Centers.* 1997.

Ronald Takaki. *Raising Cane: The World of Plantation Hawaiʻi.* 1994.

Oswald Bushnell. *The Gifts of Civilization: Germs and Genocide in Hawaiʻi.* 1993.

Dan Boylan, T. Michael Holmes. *John A. Burns: The Man and His Times.* 2000.

Kanalu Terry Young. *Rethinking the Native Hawaiian Past.* 1998.

Mahealani Uchiyama. *The Haumana Hula Handbook for Students of Hawaiian Dance.* 2016.

Rick Carroll. *IZ: Voice of the People.* 2006.

David Davis. *Waterman: The Life and Times of Duke Kahanamoku.* 2015.

Printed in Great Britain
by Amazon